IBM WEBSPHERE MQ

IBMCOOKBOOK.COM

Compiled by Terry Sanchez-Clark

IBM™ WEBSPHERE® MQ® Interview Questions

ISBN 978-1-60332-042-9

Edited By: Jamie Fisher

Printed in the United States of America

Please visit our website at www.ibmcookbook.com

Table of Contents

Introduction

IBM™ WebSphere® MQ® is a network communication technology launched by International Business Machines Corporation (IBM or Big Blue) in March 1992. It was previously known as MQSeries, which is a trademark that was rebranded by IBM in 2002 to join the suite of WebSphere products. WebSphere MQ is IBM's Message Oriented Middleware offering. It allows independent and potentially non-concurrent applications on a distributed system to communicate with each other. MQ is available on a large number of platforms (both IBM and non-IBM), including z/OS (or zero-downtime/OS, a 64-bit server operating system, also from IBM), UNIX (AIX, HP-UX, Solaris), HP NonStop, OpenVMS, Linux (a free software and open source development; its underlying source code can be freely modified, used, and redistributed by anyone) and Microsoft Windows.

There are two parts to message queuing:

Messages are collections of binary or character (for instance ASCII or EBCDIC) data that have some meaning to a participating program. As in other communications protocols, storage, routing, and delivery information is added to the message before transmission and stripped from the message prior to delivery to the receiving application.

Message queues are objects that store messages in an application.

A Queue Manager, although not strictly required for MOM, is a Websphere MQ pre-requisite and system service that provides a logical container for the message queue and is responsible for transferring data to other queue managers via message channels.

There are several advantages to this technology:

Messages do not depend on pure packet-based transmissions, such as TCP/IP. This allows the sending and receiving ends to be decoupled and potentially operate asynchronously.

Messages will be delivered once and once only, irrespective of errors and network problems.

WebSphere MQ provides assured one-time delivery of messages across a wide variety of platforms. The product emphasizes reliability and robustness of message traffic, and ensures that a message should never be lost if MQ is appropriately configured.

It needs to be remembered that a message in the context of MQ has no implication other than a gathering of data. MQ is much generalized and can be used as a robust substitute for many forms of intercommunication. For example, it can be used to implement reliable delivery of large files as a substitute for FTP (File Transfer Protocol is used to transfer data from one computer to another over the Internet or through a network)

MQ provides application designers a mechanism to achieve non-time-dependent architecture. Messages can be sent from one application to another, regardless of whether the applications are running at the same time. If a message receiver application is not running when a sender sends it a message, the queue manager will hold the message until the receiver asks for it. Ordering of all messages is preserved; by default this is in FIFO (First In, First Out) order of receipt at the local queue within priority of the message.

It provides a means for transforming data between different architectures and protocols, such as Big Endian to Little Endian, or EBCDIC to ASCII. This is accomplished through the use of message data "Exits". Exits are compiled applications, which run on the queue manager host, and are executed by the WebSphere MQ software at the time data transformation is needed.

WebSphere MQ allows receipt of messages to "trigger" other applications to run, and thus provides the framework for a message driven architecture.

It implements the Java Message Service (JMS) standard API and also has its own proprietary Application Programming Interface (API), known as the Message Queuing Interface (MQI).

Unlike email, it is MQ itself, which is responsible for determining the destination of messages by the definition of queues, so processing of sent messages can be moved to a different application at a different destination. MQ provides a robust routing architecture, allowing messages to be routed via alternative paths around a network of MQ managers. MQ can be implemented as a cluster, where multiple MQ implementations share the processing of messages to allow higher performance and load balancing.

The primary component of a WebSphere MQ installation is the Queue Manager. The queue manager handles storage, timing issues, triggering, and all other functions not directly related to actual movement of data.

Queue managers communicate with the outside world either via a direct software connection, referred to by IBM as a Bindings connection, or via a network or Client connection. The Bindings connection is limited to programs running on the same physical host as the queue manager, whereas applications using a Client connection can connect to a queue manager on any other host in the network.

Bindings connections are generally faster, but Client connections allow for a more robust, easily changeable application design. For instance, with a Client connection, the physical location of the queue manager is irrelevant, as long as it is reachable over the network.

Communication between queue managers relies on a Channel. Each queue manager uses one or more channels to send and receive data to other queue managers. A channel is uni-directional; a second channel is required to return data. In a TCP/IP based network, a channel will send or receive data on a specific port. A sending channel has a defined destination and is associated with a specific transmission queue which is the mechanism by which messages are queued awaiting transmission on the channel; a receiving channel will receive data from any other queue manager with a sending channel of the same name. When a receiving channel receives a message, it is examined to see which queue manager and queue it is destined for. In the event of a communications failure, MQ can automatically re-establish a connection when the problem is resolved.

The Listener has the function of detecting connections from incoming channels and manages the connection of the sending to the receiving channels. The Listener is the application's network interface to the queue manager. In a TCP/IP network, the Listener will "listen" for connections on a specific port.

Local queues represent the place where data is stored awaiting processing.

Remote queues represent a queue on another queue manager. It defines the destination queue, which is one element of the routing mechanism for messages.

To transmit data to a queue on another queue manager, a message is placed on a remote queue. A remote queue is sent via the temporary storage transmission queue associated with a channel. On placing a message on a remote queue, the message will be transmitted across the remote channel. If the transmission is successful the message is removed from the transmit queue. On receiving a message, the receiving queue manager will examine the message to determine whether the message is for itself or is required to forward on to another queue manager. If it is the destination, the required queue will be checked, and if it exists, the message will be placed on this queue, if not, placed on the dead letter queue. MQ has features to manage efficient transmission of data across a variety of communication mediums, so for example messages can be batched together until a queue reaches a particular depth.

Although the queue is FIFO, it is ordered based on the receipt in the local queue, not the committing of the message from the sender. Messages can be prioritized, and by default the queue is held in priority, arrival sequence. Queues will only be in sequence of addition if the message is added locally. Message grouping can be used to ensure a set of messages are in a specific order, aside from that, if sequence is critical, it is the application's responsibility to place sequence data in the message or implement a handshaking mechanism via a return queue. In reality, ordering will be maintained in straightforward configurations.

The other element of a queue manager is the log which is the mechanism used to create the robustness. As a message is placed on a queue or a configuration change is made, the data is also logged. In the event of a failure, the log is used to recreate damaged objects and recreate messages. In the event of a failure (as opposed to clean shutdown) only persistent messages will be recreated. Non-persistent messages are lost in the event of a failure or forced shutdown. Non-persistent messages can be sent across a channel, which is set to a fast mode where delivery is not assured in the event of a channel failure.

MQ is designed to support a wide variety of approaches to application development. Information can be retrieved from queues either by polling the queue to check for available data at suitable intervals, or alternatively MQ can trigger an event, allowing a client application to respond to the delivery of a message.

MQ History:
TCAM (Telecommunications Access Method) came along in 1971 with the birth of TSO. It supported asynchronous messaging, just like MQ. TCAM 3.0 added in reusable disk message queues for recovery pretty soon thereafter, just like MQ. You could write a high level PL/I program accessing TRANSIENT datasets (dynamic message queues). Read a message from a transient dataset and that message are removed from the queue, just like a non-browse READ with MQ. With the advent of computers, IBM saw an opportunity to apply new technology to the need for message switching. In the early 1960s, IBM marketed computer-like devices such as the 7740 and 7750 message switching systems.

The IBM System/360 was announced in April 1964 and with it came communication access methods such as BTAM and QTAM (Basic and Queued Telecommunications Access Methods). In the late 1960s, still another communication access method became available and it was known as TCAM, the Telecommunications Access Method. TCAM offered its users a more advanced form of message switching or message routing. TCAM was widely accepted, especially in the financial and brokerage industries.

In the late 1960s, transaction management systems came into being, each trying to achieve a leadership position in the industry. Within IBM, CICS and IMS were chosen as strategic products to address the need for transaction management. Within both CICS and IMS, each had its version of message switching, IMS being a front-end queued system and CICS having its Transient Data facility as the possible basis for message switching.

CICS established itself as a popular transaction management system in the 1968-1971 timeframe, those users who had adopted TCAM for its message handling capabilities, now wanted a combined use of TCAM with CICS. In December 1971, IBM announced CICS support of TCAM as part of the CICS/OS-Standard product, to be delivered in December 1972. For interested customers, this enabled them to use TCAM for its message handling strengths and also have TCAM-connected terminals or computers interface with CICS online applications.

In January 1973, TCAM continued to be supported by CICS/OS-Standard Version 2.3. However, TCAM support was omitted from the initial release of CICS/VS, announced in February 1973 and delivered in June 1974. Needless to say, many CICS-TCAM customers were not happy with that product direction.

With considerable pressure from CICS-TCAM customers, the CICS support of TCAM was reinstated in the CICS/VS 1.1 product, as of September 1974. In addition to the previous DCB support, with this reinstatement of TCAM support, CICS began to support TCAM access via VTAM, also known as the ACB support. CICS TCAM ACB support was discontinued as of the CICS/ESA Version 3 product in 1990.

In 1992, IBM announced a new product family called WebSphere MQ. WebSphere MQ was to be the extension of TCAM functionality from IBM-only systems to all other platforms. WebSphere MQ had an architecture that enabled heterogeneous systems to communicate with each other (e.g. IBM, HP, Sun, Tandem, etc). WebSphere MQ can be used with CICS systems to send and receive data to/from any other MQ-eligible system. WebSphere MQ can be used to initiate work in a CICS system or a CICS transaction can initiate work in another CICS or non-CICS system.

WebSphere MQ now supports 80 different environments and has become the leading message switching/routing product in the industry.

General Webshphere MQ: Operation and Maintenance of Websphere MQ systems

Question 01:
Identification/Authorization

I have an IBM Websphere MQ v6.0 queue manager running on Solaris 9. I want to prevent my staff members who have limited WebSphere MQ experience to make changes to the WMQ network.

Is there a way to do this?

A: One way is to use Dale Lane's "Using WebSphere MQ Explorer as a read-only viewer":

The WebSphere MQ Explorer GUI provides a user-friendly way to administer your queue managers. It can be used as a read-only 'viewer'. If you have some staff that doesn't have authority to make changes to the WMQ network, but need them to be able to monitor what is happening, this would let them use WMQ Explorer to do it.

The following are the steps required to set this up for a single queue manager and highlight a couple of potential problems to watch out for.

Steps to carry out on the machine hosting the queue manager:

Create a user - making sure that the user is not a member of the MQM group.
 Start a channel listener for the queue manager.
Create a server-connection (SVRCONN) channel on the queue manager - setting the MCAUSER attribute to the user name defined in step 1.
Use setmqaut to specify which objects you want the user to be able to see.

First, you need permission to connect to the queue manager:

```
setmqaut -m YOUR_QUEUE_MANAGER -t qmgr -p
YOUR_USER_NAME +connect +inq +dsp
```

Next is to give permission to the queues that WMQ Explorer will
need:

```
setmqaut -m YOUR_QUEUE_MANAGER -t q -n
SYSTEM.DEFAULT.MODEL.QUEUE -p YOUR_USER_NAME +get
+browse +inq
setmqaut -m YOUR_QUEUE_MANAGER -t q -n
SYSTEM.ADMIN.COMMAND.QUEUE -p YOUR_USER_NAME +get
+browse +inq +put
setmqaut -m YOUR_QUEUE_MANAGER -t q -n
SYSTEM.MQEXPLORER.REPLY.MODEL -p YOUR_USER_NAME +inq
+browse +get +dsp
setmqaut -m YOUR_QUEUE_MANAGER -t q -n 'AMQ.**' -p
YOUR_USER_NAME +all
setmqaut -m YOUR_QUEUE_MANAGER -t q -n 'MQAI.**' -p
YOUR_USER_NAME +all
```

Then, you could give access to all objects of a certain type, such
as being able to display all channels:

```
setmqaut -m YOUR_QUEUE_MANAGER -t channel -n '**' -p
YOUR_USER_NAME +dsp
```

You might want to include additional permissions, such as the
ability to browse messages on queues or inquire their attributes:

```
setmqaut -m YOUR_QUEUE_MANAGER -t q -n '**' -p
YOUR_USER_NAME +dsp +inq +browse
```

Review the System Administration Guide section on setmqaut
for more detail on the options available.

Steps to carry out on the WebSphere MQ Explorer machine:

Right-click on 'Queue Managers' and choose "Show Queue
Manager".
Click on the "Add" button.
Enter the queue manager name and click "Next".
Fill in the hostname of the machine hosting the queue manager,
the TCP port number for the channel listener you started and the
name of the server-connection channel you created.
Click "Finish".

Things to watch out for:

Note 1: The WebSphere MQ Explorer user will only see the objects that they have the authority to see. So it's worth being aware that in such a setup, the Explorer is no longer showing a definitive view of the objects on the queue manager.

Note 2: Attempts to view an object, which the user isn't authorized to display, can result in an authorization event. See the Monitoring WebSphere MQ section on 'Event Monitoring' (fhttp://publib.boulder.ibm.com/infocenter/wmqv6/v6r0/index .jsp?topic=/com.ibm.mq.csqzax.doc/monevent.htm) for more information. To summarize, if a queue manager has authorization events (AUTHOREV) enabled, every attempt to access something which a user is not authorized to will cause an event message to be put to the SYSTEM.ADMIN.QMGR.EVENT queue. So, for example, if a user does not have access to display queues, then one authorization event message will be put to SYSTEM.ADMIN.QMGR.EVENT for each queue they cannot access every time the Queues view in WMQ Explorer is refreshed. This could result in a lot of messages, so you may want to disable AUTHOREV or take steps to handle these messages.

Note 3: If you want to look at queues with WebSphere MQ Explorer in this way, you will need to have Refresh Pack 6.0.2.0 or greater applied. A bug in the Explorer prior to this meant that the failure to display SYSTEM.AUTH.DATA.QUEUE (a queue which it is not possible to give a non-mqm user access to) prevented any queues from being displayed. This is documented more fully in APAR IC49051 (http://www-1.ibm.com/support/docview.wss?rs=171&uid=swg1IC49051)

Note 4: When I talk about the WMQ Explorer, I'm referring to the Eclipse-based Explorer that comes with WebSphere MQ version 6. I've not tried this on the v5.3 Windows WMQ Explorer.

Note 5: In the examples above, we used the -p option for setmqaut - specifying a specific user. This was done for simplicity but in practice using -g to specify a group is often easier to manage. See the System Administrative Guide for the full syntax.

Question 02: Websphere MQ & DB2 MQListener

I have a system that receives a message and calls a DB2 stored procedure to process it via a db2mqlsn command (on Windows). Now I'm migrating the system to Linux and the only thing left for me to do, is to setup the db2mqls to start automatically after the MQ manager starts.

My problem is that running the command won't return a result because it keeps running indefinitely. Here's part of what I got on the script (on /etc/init.d/):

```
su - mqm -c "cd /opt/mqm/bin; ./strmqm MYQUEUEMANAGER "
su - db2inst1 -c "cd /opt/ibm/db2/V9.1/bin; ./db2mqlsn run -configDB MYDB -config mydbconfig"
```

How can I setup a command call like that in the script that I have created that starts my MQ manager at boot (on /etc/init.d/)?

A: You might want to put the command into the background. At the end of the command just put a '&':

```
Code:
runmqlsr -m MYQMGR -t tcp -p 1414 &
```

Question 03: Get support from IBM for MQ5.3 for Tandem Nonstop

What's the best way to file problem reports about version 5.3 of MQ for Tandem Nonstop systems?

I have access to IBMLINK, what is the "Software Component Id" that should be used for the Tandem based 5.3 products? I have tried all of the numbers I have found in the documentation and in the read me files and none of them work.

A: Try using 5724A39. Also, you should try the ESR interface to IBM for the Tandem.

ESR will allow you to generate a PMR (case) but like all things, you need to be authorized by your companies IBM services coordinator.

Question 04: Saving change impact on MQ

We are running 5.2 and 5.3. Our servers had the MS DST patches applied and the server OS time was correct; however, Eclipse was still showing times that is one hour behind.

Does day light saving change has any impact on MQ application?

A: Customers need to ensure that the JRE being used by eclipse that can be customized by customers is up to date by running the JTZU against the specified version that they are using. The actions that need to be taken are as follows:

1. Identify the JDK in use by eclipse. This can be done launching the WebSphere MQ explorer and then following the menu tree:

Window ->Preferences -> Java -> Installed JREs

A list of one or more installed JREs is displayed in the panel. One of these JREs will be "checked" indicating that it is the one that eclipse will use to run Java code (MQ Explorer in this case) against. Make a note of this location for example C:\JDK\J150 - Download and extract the appropriate JTZU from:

http://www-128.ibm.com/developerworks/java/jdk/dst/index.html

2. Use the command and change directories to the extract location.

3. Alter the runjtzuenv.bat file to set the location of a JVM that the tool will be launched under. For example:

```
rem set JAVA_HOME to the a Java installation
directory
set JAVA_HOME=c:\jdk\j142\jre
rem set NOGUI
set NOGUI=false
rem set DISCOVERONLY
set DISCOVERONLY=true
rem set SILENTPATCH
set SILENTPATCH=false
```

This would instruct the tool to run against a JRE (in this case 1.4.2) at a location c:\jdk\j142\jre:

- Launch the tool using runjtzu.bat
- Select 'Interactive mode' and click start button
- Ensure customer make a note of the warning message regarding applying maintenance
- Enter the location of the java runtime being used by eclipse, for example c:\jdk\J150\jre (please note that '\jre' is needed here)
- Click update to begin the update process.

Customer should then re-test the MQExplorer and determine if the problem persists.

Question 05: FDC Files filling up the disk space

We are using the MQ version 5.3 with the CSD Version 5 in Windows Server 2000. Since last 2 weeks, the FDC files are being generated continuously and now have occupied the drive completely. We have deleted some old FDC to free some space.

How do I stop these FDCs' from getting generated?

A: This one's from IBM:

Problem:
You are running WebSphere® MQ v5.3. You monitor MQ with a user developed shell script, which runs runmqsc every 10 minutes. This script produces FDC files for probe id XC076001 and reason code of xecX_E_CONV_NOT_SUP. These FDC files also are reporting "Cat CCSID 954, user CCSID 819". This means that the message catalog is using CCSID 954. The FDC does not stop runmqsc or the script. The environment where the messages come from is the one issuing the runmqsc commands and is also using CCSID 819.

Cause:
This problem occurs because you have LC_ALL set to blank or no value. In this case the value of LC_ALL= will take precedence over LANG. So the default locale, English 819, is taken. Since there is no conversion table for 950 to 819 available the message display fails.

Solution:
Set LC_ALL=ja and export this in a shell. Issue locale command and this should display LANG and LC_* as "ja". Once the display shows the values correctly, issue runmqsc and check if the problem is resolved.

Also, it is suggested that you set all locale variables to the same value. In this case, either set them all to be "ja" or set all to be Japanese.

The locale output for the failing machine shows:

```
LANG=ja
LC_CTYPE=japanese
LC_NUMERIC="ja"
LC_TIME="ja"
LC_COLLATE="ja"
LC_MONETARY="ja"
LC_MESSAGES=japanese
LC_ALL=
```

Question o6: Connection B/W MQ running on SOLARIS and Z/OS

We installed MQ Server 5.3 on a SUN Solaris Host. How would I create a connection b/w Solaris MQ and Mainframe MQ? Is there any file in which I need to give the IP address of remote host?

A: You need to create MQ channels between the two queue managers. Two manuals to look at: MQ Intercommunications and MQ Script Command Reference.

Briefly, channels come in pairs; one Sender and one Receiver, for example:
Messages flow one way on a channel. If you need messages to flow in the other direction, you will need to create a second pair of channels. Sender channels send messages from a transmission queue (xmitq). The QRemote definition specifies the name of the xmit queue. The programmer opens the QRemote definition.

To get messages from SUN to z/OS, create:

On the SUN qmgr: one Sender channel from SUN to z/OS. Let's call it SUN.ZOS. On the Sender channel definition you specify ipaddress (port) of the z/OS qmgr and listener.

On z/OS: one Receiver channel from SUN to z/OS. Exact same name: SUN.ZOS.

To get messages from z/OS to SUN, create the inverse channel pair. Let's call it ZOS.SUN:

On z/OS: one Sender channel from z/OS to SUN, specifying SUN qmgr ipaddress (port).

On SUN: one Receiver channel from z/OS to SUN. Exact same channel name: ZOS.SUN.

Examples for each platform type are in the Intercommunications manual.

You will need to have IP running on both SUN and z/OS and you will need to have listeners running on both, as well.

Question 07: Unsubscribing topic with command

We have a situation where we need to unsubscribe a topic in Publish Subscribe setup. The same is not working through our program. Can we issue any command that can be used to unsubscribe a topic or all the topics?

A: Send an "unsubscribe" message with RFHUtil or similar. Another option is to delete the subscription through the broker admin interface.

Question 08: Same message consumed by two different application

We have three qmgrs QM1, QM2 & QM3 which are connected to three applications App1 to QM1, App2 to QM2, & App3 to QM3. The requirement is to have messages sent by App1 to QM2 (Distributed Queing). This message has to be consumed by App2 from QM2 and also the same message has to be sent to QM3 to be consumed by App3.

The app team informed us that there won't be any change in the code so we have to get this done only with MQ. Is this achievable using MQ?

A: Try the mirrorq exit. Please bear in mind the mirrorq exit is sample code & not necessarily production strength. If you're going to use this over anything other than the short term, review it and be sure you're confident of its robustness and your ability to support it.

Question 09: MQ update DB on another computer

From Machine A, a client program sends a request to MQ server in Machine B. Now, that computer updates the DB situated in another Machine C. Is this possible only with triggering?

A: Your scenario relies on Machine A being able to place a request message on Machine B, hence you'd need an MQ client connection between A and B or server side channels to carry the message. Machine B must be able to access the database on Machine C, so this implies a client link between the two machines. Unless they have replicated databases, RPC links, piped data transfer or an MQ link running PM4Data.

You would also need a triggered application on Machine B unless the application on Machine B was written to be long running or there wasn't an application on Machine B. This could only be written in Java or C or a language with a supported environment on Machine B, unless there wasn't an application at all.

Question 10: SSL certificate selection

I am having a queue manager to whom 10 different applications connects. I want to make them connect over SSL svrconn channels and for them to represent different unique certificates. So all 10 application key repositories will have same queue manager certificate but my queue manager key repository will have 10 different certificates, one from each application.

My question is how queue manager will know which certificate to use for handshake when a connection request comes?

A: QMGR will use their cert from keystore which alias name is Ibmwebspheremq<qmgr_name_lowercase> during handshake.

Then in your configuration QMGR compares sent application public certificate with certificates from keystore.

Consider using standard PKI with CA rather than self-signed cert.

Question 11: Max message size overhead

What is the overhead on MQ for having a large value for maximum message length in a queue definition?

For example, if I define the maximum message length to say 10MB but the maximum message length is only initially set at 1MB.

Can this affect any performance on the settings else where?

A: The space used to hold the value for MaxMsgLen is a constant; it's the same no matter what number is used for MaxMsgLen.

The only way that, for example, setting the MaxMsgLn for all queues, channels and qmgrs to the maximum possible will have any performance impact is if your logs are not sized to handle that size of message AND someone actually SENDS a big message.

Set it to the largest value you can possibly handle, and then you don't have to worry about changing it every time an application needs a bigger value. Setting the MaxMsgLn doesn't affect anything else. Sending a large message does.

Max Message length is only a safety feature to not receive unexpectedly large message.

Question 12: Create Qmgr in Explorer (V6)

How does WMQ Explorer (V6) communicate with the local MQ to create the Qmgr? My understanding is it uses client code to remotely administer already running Qmgrs. Obviously, the client cannot be used before the QMgr is created and running. I am interested in both Windows and UNIX platforms.

A: To create QMGR MQ 6 Explorer just use standard commands:

```
Code:
crtmqm   QMGR
amqmdain qmgr start QMGR
```

Click "Show details" button when you are creating QMGR from toolkit and you will see it.

Question 13: Queue option field not available

My MQ Explorer interface shows an option that is not shown at the MQExplorer help. It seems to be pretty similar to the "Disconnect Interval" (DISCINT) but shows a different range of options ("Auto" or 0 to 999..99).

The issue is that besides not finding what it does mean on the online help, I can only provide you with a close translation, since my MQExplorer detects my country language and provides all text captions in Portuguese.

It is something like "Interval to maintain active". Has anyone an idea of what is the English equivalent or the MQ short name for it?

A: KAINT, Keep Alive Interval.

Question 14: Trigger monitor error after migrating to MQ6.0.2

We migrated from MQ5.3 to MQ6.02 and this is on HP-UX Itanium. I have started a trigger monitor after migrating to MQ6.0.2 but receive the following error message:

```
Waiting for a trigger message

/spare/dman/bin/cdborcv 'TMC 2CDB.MACHINERY.UPDATE.Q
CDB.MACHINERY.UPDATE.P /spare/dman/bin/cdborcv &
/spare/dman/ini/MACH.ini A.CMDB.QMGR ' &
/usr/lib/dld.sl: Can't open shared library:
/usr/lib/libmqm.sl
/usr/lib/dld.sl: No such file or directory
End of application trigger.

CDB.MATCH.REQUEST.P is triggered when messages hit
CDB.MATCH.REQUEST.Q.
CDB.MATCH.REQUEST.P should then run
/spare/dman/bin/cdborcv which using IPC and MQ
details held in /spare/dman/ini/MAT1.ini to move the
MQ message to the IPC queue.
MAT1.ini points to an error log
/spare/dman/errlog/MAT1.log.
```

Therefore, it looks like cdborcv is not being triggered. I have checked /usr/lib and cannot find libmqm.sl. However, libmqm.so exists. The application which is triggered is written in C. The application is quite old and wouldn't be 64bit. Would re-compiling it against the version 6 libraries possibly work?

A: At 5.3, the only HP WMQ server was PA_RISC; at 6.0 there is PA-RISC & Itanium. The programs are not compatible between the two.

Your application is compiled PA-RISC. On WMQ HP PA-RISC, the shared libraries have the suffix .sl. On Itanium, the suffix is .so. You have to recompile your application.

Question 15: Error Code 2082

I have an MQ cluster with two queue managers QM_A and QM_B. QM_B act as the gateway into the cluster and all connection must pass thru QM_B as this is where we implement our security checks.

An application connection to QM_B over MQ client connection: This application is a 3rd party product over which we have no control. Messages arrive to a queue local on QM_B from QM_A. The application is designed to poll this queue on QM_B and then send responses back to QM_A via a queue alias. Thus;

QA (alias on QM_A for request) -----> QL (clustered queue on QM_B for request)

QL (clustered queue on QM_A for Resp) <--- QA (alias on QM_B for Resp)

All queue objects are defined with the attribute DEFBIND (NOTFIXED). When the application tries to open the queue on QM_B, I get the error code 2082, suggesting that MQ is trying to resolve the target on the local queue manager, QM_B. However, this should be being resolved over the cluster to the QM_A.

I suspect the application is opening the queue alias using code like this;

```
MQQueue q = qmgr.accessQueue ("QA on QM_B",
openOption, "QM_B", null, null);
```

I am getting the error code 2082 (MQRC_UNKNOWN_ALIAS_BASE_Q) when trying to resolve a queue local over a cluster. What is causing this error?

A: The response is best left without any aliases. The application on QM_B should just send the response to the qmgr and queue as stated in the reply to fields of the request. The requestor specifies the qmgr and queue name it wants the reply be sent to. This "reply to" queue does not need to be clustered.

Cluster resolution will only come into play for the routing from QM_B to QM_A and should not play any role with the queue resolution. Remember the replyto queue could be a temporary dynamic queue...

You are only talking about 2 qmgrs but the typical scenario here would have clustered clones of QM_B for load balancing.

Question 16: Triggering a new application

I want to start a windows service whenever a new message is put in to the queue by one application (.net application). Is it possible to trigger a service whenever a new message arrives at the Queue manager?

A: Windows service is a long running task started at machine boot. Technically, it's a straightforward task to have an MQ process start a service as a process can do anything a command prompt can do. You'd just need the trigger process to have Administrator rights on the Windows machine; something your IT audit & security people may have a view on.

Question 17: amqcrsta

Is there a way to confirm if an amqcrsta process is still valid or orphaned?

A: Yes, first get a list of the amqcrsta processes that Websphere MQ knows are active.

1. Start the script command processor with runmqsc qmrgname.
2. Enter dis chs(*) JOBNAME.
3. Enter end to end the script command processor.

Note: If the resulting list is long, redirect the list to a file with the command echo dis chs(*) JOBNAME | runmqsc qmgrname > list.out. Compare this list with all existing amqcrsta processes.

   * On Windows/NT/2000/XP, open the task manager and click on the Processes tab to get the active amqcrsta processes. The process ID is listed in the PID column. You can click on Image Name to sort the list.

   * On UNIX, enter ps -ef | grep amqcrsta to get the active amqcrsta processes.

Compare each of the PIDs with the list generated from runmqsc. The PID is the first 8 bytes of the JOBNAME field. If a PID appears in the process list but not in the runmqsc JOBNAME list, it is an orphaned process.

Question 18: Analyze open input count of a local queue

We are working on TIBCO-CIM (Master data management Tool). The product has standard inbound queue (Q_STD). We have work flow which will process the message put in that std queue.

As per requirement, I have created 2 custom queues for inbound (Q_A, Q_B). When I start the CIM server after adding creating these two queues, the open input count of custom queue shows up a random num Q_A - 37 and Q_B-31. When I restart the server, it just varies in a random way, open input count for Q_A - 54 and Q_B-1.

Now I deleted the custom queue. When I restart the server, the open input count for Q_STD (std queue) is 394.

Only one workflow is designed to process the message from that queue. I couldn't list the connection names as I'm working with v5.x. Is there any other way to find what might be the reason for such high value for open input count?

A: Here is a basic Perl script to analyze the output: amqldmpa -m <qmgr name> -c K -f /tmp/qm.txt and then use the script below with qm.txt on the command line:

```
Code:
#! /usr/bin/perl -w
#
# Goes through QMgr connection dump and formats it.
#
#
#   Who     When       What
#   dgoldin 07.06.07   Initial coding.
#
$FNam = $ARGV[0];
open (FH, $FNam) or die "Can't open $FNam: $! ";
while (<FH>)
{
    if ( /ApplPid:/ )
    {
        $ApplPid = substr($_, 26, 7);
    }
```

```
    if ( /ApplName:/ )
    {
        $ApplName = substr($_, 26, 40);
    }
    if ( /UserContext/ )
    {
        $UserId = substr($_, 26, 8);
        write;

    }
    if ( /ObjectName:/ )
    {
        $ObjectName = substr($_, 26, 64);
        print "     ",$ObjectName;
    }
}
close (FH);

format STDOUT =
@<<<<<< @>>>>>>>>>>>>>>>>>>>>>>>>>>>>>>>>>>>>>>>>>
@>>>>>>>>>
$ApplPid, $ApplName, $UserId
```

Question 19: MSA User ID behavior

I'm in the process of setting up intercommunication between our organization and a business partner. In the interest of controlling the access to a specific QManager and Queue in our environment, I flipped the Put Authority to Context on our receive channel and Set the MCA User Id to an internally known account. Subsequently, I've secured the Qmanager and Queue as tightly as reasonable using this account.

The channel starts fine but when our business partner sends a message, it goes to dead letter in the context of an account they are using basically because it's not secured to put on the application queue. My expectation was that the context would change to the MCA user even on the put.

I am also implementing BlockIP as a security exit. Do I need to create a mirrored account and secure it?

A: If you set the channel Put Authority to ctx (context) like you did, this is exactly what happens. The userid in the mqmd of the message is used to put to the queue and since it doesn't exist in your environment it is not authorized to do so.

Setting the MCAUSER on the channel has no effect in this situation.

In order for it to work as you expect, you do not want the channel "putaut" set to "ctx".

Question 20: Messages delay

I'm using MQ 5.3 CSD 10 on Windows Server 2003. I have a trigger queue which I would like to delay the messages on it for 15 minutes before they get pulled by the application. Is there a way to do it on the MQ/Queue level without having to write a program or change the application itself?

A: Put the original message with MD.Report set to MQRO_EXPIRATION_WITH_FULL_DATA and an expiration time of 1800 (15 minutes worth of half-seconds). When the message expires after the required 15 minutes, the report message is written to the MD.ReplyQ. If this queue is triggered, the application can then get the message from there.

Question 21: Ten Commandments of MQSeries

Normally, when we get the message from the server through an application (vb, net windows application), that message will be automatically get removed from the Queue. As per my requirement (Wmq version 6.0), I want to hold the messages in the Queue even after the message is get() and clear the messages later.

Is there any property that needs to be changed to accomplish that?

A: Do not bother when MQ does this for you. Browsing is very seldom a good idea for an application program.

Here are the Ten Commandments of MQSeries:

Thou shall not use a queue as a database.
Thou shall backup your page sets, file systems and logs.
Thou shall routinely apply maintenance to your MQ Series systems.
Thou shall use MQCLOSE and MQDISC when terminating an application.
Thou shall not use MQGET with WAIT UNLIMITED without specifying MQGMO_FAIL_IF_QUIESCING.
Thou shall not create objects with long and drawn out names.
Thou shall create standard naming conventions.
Thou shall provide systems management tools for administrators and users.
Thou shall not create an MQ Series network without mapping out all connections and object relations on paper first.
Thou shall not attempt to apply asynchronous methods to all problems simply because MQ Series is a wonderful product.

Question 22: Maximum message length

I am using MQ server V 6.0.0.0. Is there any way to increase the Maximum Message length for the Queue manager?

A: Maximum message length is parameter of queue, channel and QMGR. You can change it with MQSC script or with GUI.

Another way is using segmentation when you don't have enough memory to process huge message.

More specifically, the maximum size of a physical message is 100Meg. This is the maximum message length that can be put/get.

A logical message (composed of one or more physical messages) can be as big as you want.

Question 23: COA & COD

My organization is on one end on an MQ and we send messages to an MQ on the other end. The messages are certificates which are generated by an application on our side. The problem is that the recipient of our certificates claims that they receive some of them outside the time frame allowed. Naturally, the easiest way to address this issue is for the recipient to send some kind of acknowledgement to us when they receive our message but they refuse to do this.

Is it possible to extract a log which shows when messages arrived on our queue and when they left our queue?

A: I suggest that you use both COA & COD report messages and create a simple SLA database. Try these steps:

Create a database with 6 or more columns: transaction key / name, MsgId, CorrelId (if non null), put time, COA time and COD time. You can use any DB. i.e. Oracle, MySQL, Cloudscape, ..

For all messages sent to the 'client', set the COA & COD report options and set a 'Reply-To-Q' (if you are not using one).

If you have a unique transaction key / id / name then store it in a MQMD field. Suggestions are: CorrelId or ApplicationIdData.

If you don't have an application reading messages from the 'Reply-To-Q' then create one and it will:
Determine if the message is COA or COD.
Retrieve the necessary information from the MQMD.
Insert a record into the DB.

Now, when a client complains about delayed messages, you can search the DB for particular record and provide / prove if the transaction was truly late.

The best information is the difference in the message times between the COA and COD. It will tell you how long the message sat in THEIR queue before they picked it up.

There is nothing better than a client complaining and then you say "but why did it sit in your queue for 4 minutes and 33 seconds".

Question 24: RFHUTILC & Set User Id

I'm using RFHUTILC (C) V 4.2.0, build 187 (Sept 72006) on Win XP against multiple servers. I can connect with no problem the first one but I get a 2035 authorization failure against the second one. I use the same Id for each different password between machines.

I am concerned that the Set User Id dialog isn't saving the Id correctly. Regardless of what I put in the security section, it will still connect to the first machine.

The first server is AIX and the second one is Solaris. What could be happening here?

A: You could use the RUNAS option and create a local Id to match the one you want to run against. In many cases the password is not checked at the queue manager end.

Unless you or your MQ Admin has implemented a security solution on those remote queue managers then MQ ignores the User Id and Password sent in the MQCSP security structure. Hence, when you connect to the remote queue manager via RFHUTILC, the installed MQ Client code is retrieving your Windows logged on User Id and sending it to the remote queue manager regardless of what you put in the security section.

Therefore, one of 2 things is happening:

The SVRCONN channel has an authorized UserId in the MCAUSER field of the channel.
Or your Windows UserId is authorized to one system but not to the other.

Question 25: Get acknowledgement

I want to send some XML file as a message to queue, get ack*
from MQ Series and then show the acknowledgement in some
message box for user. This is to be sure the message is received
in the queue.

Can I do this programmatically? If not, what methods should I
use in my application?

A: You don't get an acknowledgement/ack. You'll get a
completion code and a reason code. If the completion code
indicates failure, the reason code will tell you why.

Typically if the message is successfully put, it's taken that it will
reach its destination. This is the essence of the assured delivery
WMQ offers.

If you're using an object oriented API (java, .net) you might not
get a reason or completion code from the PUT. You'll just fail to
get an exception, so only write NEGATIVE if you get an
exception.

Question 26: Memory leak in MQLQMAG

IBM has identified a memory leak in MQLQMAG (fixed in CSD03). I have several running instances of this object and one in particular is consuming almost 1GB of SWAP. Can this process be stopped without any adverse impact to the Queue Manager? Basically what is this process used for?

A: The MQLQMAG is the relation MQ==> Local application for APIs (MQGET,MQPUT,MQINQ,....)

If you stop a MQLQMAG process the application connected by this one received a 2009. No other problems with the rest of processes.

Quote from the manual:
The Local Queue Manager Agents (LQMA) performs the operations required to process MQI calls on behalf of applications. The Agents execute the bulk of the code that supports the MQI. The primary purpose of the agent is to separate application programs from the queue manager's critical resources, to protect against rogue or malicious applications. The number of agent processes depends on the number of connected applications and the MinIdleLQMAgents specified in the QMINI file. When the queue manager starts, each execution controller will start the specified number of idle agents. As agents become active, the Execution Controller starts new agents to maintain the minimum number of idle agents.

Question 27: Dead letter queue

From .Net Application, I want to put message in to a dead letter Queue if there is any problem in the message. I want to see all the messages that are there in the DLQ at the end of the day from my .net application. Is this advisable?

A: Do not use the system dead letter queue for application messages with a problem. It's designed for use where the queue manager has a problem with messages. If you are going to use it you can just put to it like any normal queue, but ensure that the messages you add & populate a dead letter header as described in the Application Programming Reference manual. Without this none of the DLQ handling tools will work.

You're much better advised to create your own local queue (MY.PROBLEMS or similar) and code your application to write to that in the event of problem. You will find the Backout queue and count attributes on the queue useful in this regard.

Question 28: Server connection channel

I wrote a Java program to connect to the qmgr in client mode using the Channel SYSTEM.DEF.SVRCONN.

I was able to post messages to queue and everything was working fine. I like to know whether the server connection channel "SYSTEM.DEF.SVRCONN " was actually used in posting the message to the queue.

The status of SYSTEM.DEF.SVRCONN was inactive after posting the message. I expected it to be running. Like sender channels used to trigger receiver channels, I expected serverCONN channels to be triggered by clientCONN channels. Was this actually happening?

A: The svrconn channel is only active the time between connect and disconnect of the qmgr. So if your connect post and disconnect is really quick you might not even see the difference in the svrconn channel status.

Try to comment the line in the java code where you say:

```
Code:
MQEnvironment.channel="SYSTEM.DEF.SVRCONN" and then
recompile and try to put the message...
```

You can look at the message count of the channel using "dis chs(mychl) saved". Or you can set the MCAUSER of the channel to some user that does not exists and see if anyone comes to ask why they're getting a 2035 all of a sudden.

Question 29: FIRST trigger type

If the trigger type is FIRST, does it mean that the trigger is fired only for the very first message on the queue when it is created or for every first message whenever the queue is empty?

If the later is true, then can we safely assume that trigger type FIRST is same as trigger type DEPTH with depth 1?

A: TRIGTYPE=FIRST is the default. When the number of messages on the triggered queue goes from zero to one, the queue is triggered, the queue manager creates a trigger message and places it on the initiation queue and then trigger monitor reads that message and starts the program. It is also the recommended practice for quite a long time because it's the option that works the best and fits the best into MQ design patterns.

Trigtype(first) and all the usual stuff for triggering the trigint will come to play in the following situation:

The queue is not empty. The queue is not serviced. A new message hits the queue. If that message is in the interval (last trigger msg + trigint) there is no trigger message generated.

If the new message is outside the interval (last trigger msg + trigint), a new trigger message is generated.

If there is no new message hitting the queue and the interval is greater than trigint since the last trigger message there is no trigger message generated. The generation of a new trigger message is dependent on the event: a message is put to the queue + evaluation of trigint

TRIGTYPE=DEPTH: When the depth of the queue goes from one less than TRIGDPTH to equal to TRIGDPTH, the queue is triggered and the process continues as in TRIGTYPE=FIRST.

However for a TRIGTYPE of DEPTH, when the trigger conditions are satisfied on the triggered queue, the queue manager creates a trigger message and disables triggering on that queue using the TriggerControl attribute. The triggered application must re-enable triggering itself by using the MQSET call.

Also, the trigger interval (TRIGINT) attribute of the queue manager comes into picture when TRIGTYPE is FIRST.

Usage of TRIGINT as per IBM docs:

"When the arrival of a message on a queue causes a trigger message to be put on the initiation queue, then any message that arrives on the same queue within the specified interval does not cause another trigger message to be put on the initiation queue"

The trigint is used to prevent unnecessary triggering of applications. If you use trigtype as depth then the qmgr turns off the triggering to prevent unwanted triggering. But now the application needs to set it back to turn on triggering. This is not required if you are using trigtype(FIRST).

Question 30: Error 2058

I'm running 2 MQ servers (5.3) on two PCs with windows, using AMI for C++.

My application on the first PC needs to connect both to local queues and connect as a client to the remote server. I've created an AMQCLCHL.tab file which points to the second server.

When I connect (open the AMI session) to the local queue manager first and then to the remote one, the remote connection fails, giving me MQ error 2058. I'm assuming that it is trying to connect to the queue manager at the local host, ignoring the tab file.

When I connect to the remote one first, it connects and works but then when I connect to the local one, it seems to connect (no exception is thrown) but my sent message does not appear on the queue. What could be the cause of the error?

A: You need to connect to both qmgrs as a client, regardless of the fact that one is a local qmgr. This means you need to specify your connection with hostname, channel, and port.

Probably, the AMI is deciding that you want to use a binding connection if you connect to the local qmgr first.

Make sure your V5.3 is running at CSD13. It's best to switch to using XMS instead of AMI.

Installation and Configuration: Installing and configuring Websphere MQ for any platform

Question 31: MCATYPE(THREAD)

We have a MQ Server (AIX platform, V6) that has to receive thousands of MQCONNX() from remote MQ Client stations.

When we saw "MCATYPE(THREAD)", we thought we had found a way to increase the number of possible connections but it is ONLY AVAILABLE for SDR, SVR, and RQSTR (plus cluster).

How is it is not available for SVRCONN channels ?

A: SVRCONNS aren't used for "outgoing" connections; they're used for "incoming" connections. So the quote on MCATYPE: "Specifies whether the message-channel-agent program on an outbound MCA channel should run as a thread or a process"

This is why it's not applicable to SVRCONNs.

The documentation on this channel parameter goes on to say:

"In situations where a threaded listener is required to service a large number of incoming requests, resources can become strained. In this case, you should use multiple listener processes and target incoming requests at specific listeners though the port number specified on the listener"

If you're running out of processes on an AIX box, you should not be considering using it for a high-volume client concentrator.

Question 32: Set up queues and communication between RS6000 and Windows Client

We have recently started using MQ Series and are having some problems setting up communication between our RS6000 server and Windows 2000 client.

After installing we set up the following on the RS6000:

Queue called QUEUE.DEFAULT
Queue manager called QUEUE.MANAGER.DEFAULT

Using the following commands:

```
crtmqm -q queue.manager.default
strmqm
runmqsc
define qlocal (queue.default)
end
```

We then tested that we could put and get messages from the queue locally using:

```
./amqsput QUEUE.DEFAULT and ./amqsget QUEUE.DEFAULT
```

This worked fine and we could see the messages we put onto the queue without any problems. We then set up a channel using:

```
define channel (channel1) chltype (svrconn)
trptype(tcp) mcauser ('mqm')
```

and on the Windows machine set the Environment variable:

```
SET MQSERVER=CHANNEL1/TCP/192.168.100.29
```

Where 192.168.100.29 is the RS6000's IP Address (can be pinged using this).

However when we run the following commands:

```
amqsputc QUEUE.DEFAULT QUEUE.MANAGER.DEFAULT
amqsputc QUEUE.DEFAULT
```

We get the following output each time:

```
Sample AMQSPUT0 start
MQCONN ended with reason code 2059
```

We also set up another channel as a receiver channel using:

"define channel (channel2) chltype(rcvr) trptype(tcp)" and altered the Windows environment variable to reflect this.

However we still get the same error message. We haven't changed any of the default communication ports, so it should be using TCP port 1414. What have we missed?

A: In WebSphere MQ v 6.0 the listeners automatically created are set to "manual" start. You would need to either change/start the listener:

```
alter listener(SYSTEM.DEFAULT.LISTENER.TCP)
trptype(tcp) control(qmgr)
```

Or just start it each time :

```
start listener(SYSTEM.DEFAULT.LISTENER.TCP)
```

Or you can start a new one from a command prompt (which applies to WebSphere MQ 5.3) :

```
runmqlsr -t tcp -m QUEUE.MANAGER.DEFAULT -p 1414
```

If you have the listener running then you got a firewall running.

Question 33: Installing MQ in Ubuntu 7.04

I've tried to install MQ 6 in an Ubuntu 7.04 dev machine unzipping the IBM's C8472ML.tar.gz file.

I have alien and rpm installed because all install files are rpm based. Unfortunately, when I try to install the runtime: $ sudo alien -idc MQSeriesRuntime-6.0.0-0.i386.rpm

I get this message:

"[: 51: upgrade: bad number chown: cannot access `/usr/share /locale /C /LC_MESSAGES /amq.cat': any such file or directory"

How do I go around this problem?

A: Install the rpms (Runtime, Server at least) using 'rpm -ivh --nodeps '. Before doing anything else, install the latest fixes since crtmqm does not work at the base level (AMQ8101).

Question 34: Strange MQ issue on Win2000 server

We are using MQ v5.3 CSD06 on Win2000 platform. We setup a Trigger Monitor service using the MQ services GUI. The Triggering works fine until the box is rebooted. Upon server restart, Triggering does not work since the Trigger Monitor settings are not carried across the server re-start. The issue is not consistent though, sometimes the Trigger Monitor service itself is missing post-restart. Sometimes the InitQ for the Trigger Monitor service just gets blanked out.

Why is the server not persistent across server boots?

A: This is a known issue with CSD06. You should upgrade to CSD13.

Question 35: Can't see Queue Manager in MQ Explorer

After migrating from MQ 5.3 on Windows 2003 to MQ 6 using the latest service pack, the queue manager is running fine from the command line. However, I don't see the queue manager when I bring up the MQ Explorer.

I try to add it manually but it is being treated as a remote queue manager while it is actually a local queue manager. I was prompted for the hostname and port. What can possibly cause this problem?

A: From the command line, issue to following command:

```
strmqcfg -i
```

Then this code:

```
strmqcfg -c
```

This will delete any cached data used by the Eclipse runtime.

Question 36: Check existence of QMgr

Is it possible to check if the queue manager exists or not on the box by using scripts? I want to run a script for creating QMgr and queues. But before I run this script, I want to check if the queue manager exists. If it exists, I want the script to exit.

A: To find out if Qmgr is running:

On Solaris/AIX:

```
Code:
#!/usr/bin/ksh
dspmq | grep -v Running | cut -d '(' -f2,3 | cut -d
')' -f1 | while read qmgr
do
   status=`dspmq -m $qmgr | cut -d '(' -f2,3 | cut -d
')' -f2 | cut -d '(' -f2`
   echo QMgr $qmgr is $status
done
```

On Windows:

```
Code:
for /F "tokens=1,2,3,4,5,* delims=()" %i IN ('dspmq')
DO @IF NOT %l==Running echo QMgr %j is %l
```

Above scripts already ignore Running qmgrs; replace the "echo ..." statement with the action you want to "perform".

Here are some variations:

To execute a command against all Running QMgrs:

On Solaris/AIX:

```
Code:
#!/usr/bin/ksh
dspmq | grep Running | cut -d '(' -f2,3 | cut -d ')'
-f1 | while read qmgr
do
   command_to_execute $qmgr
done
```

On Windows:

```
Code:
for /F "tokens=1,2,3,4,5,* delims=()" %i IN ('dspmq')
DO @IF %1==Running command_to_excute %j
```

Execute a command against all QMgrs:

On Solaris/AIX:

```
Code:
#!/usr/bin/ksh
dspmq | cut -d '(' -f2,3 | cut -d ')' -f1 | while
read qmgr
do
    command_to_execute $qmgr
done
```

On Windows:

```
Code:
for /F "tokens=1,2,3,4,5,* delims=()" %i IN ('dspmq')
DO command_to_excute %j
```

Question 37: Compile programs using Cygwin

I have a program currently running on AIX 5.1 using MQ Client libraries which I'd like to run on windows under cygwin.

I can compile & link my program if I copy over the include (WebSphere MQ\Tools\c\include) & lib (WebSphere MQ\Tools\Lib) files from my windows server install into my cygwin (/usr/mqm/include and /usr/mqm/lib respectively). The problem is at runtime, I don't know where to put my channel table. The program reports a 2058 error.

A: The location of the channel table is controlled by an environment variable MQCHLLIB (and its name by MQCHLTAB). Without these, the default location is the root of the MQ install.

You might be able to make it work using the libs (put channel table under the "c:\program files\IBM\Websphere MQ" directory) but you could get any kind of problem & the configuration would be unsupported.

If you want a program to achieve client access to the queue manager, you need to install the client product (which is free of license). Get the free Microsoft Windows 'C' compiler that is supported by IBM and compile and link your program as a native Win32 application.

Question 38: Install MQ v6.0 on a different filesystem

Is it possible to install MQ V6.0 for Aix 5.2 on a different filesystem? By default, it goes to /var/mqm. Can I install it on /test for instance? Can I create a symbolic link for /var/mqm?

A: You can not change the paths that MQ will use internally. This means that a path "/var/mqm" has to exist. Where the filesystem that path points to is irrelevant.

Don't forget that the installation also puts symlinks in /usr/lib and /usr/bin and installs the message catalogs in /usr/lib/nls/msg and that install itself keeps its package data in /usr/lpp/mqm*, /usr/lib/objrepos and /etc/objrepos. If you are trying to do an installation without touching /usr or without disturbing an existing installation it will be very difficult.

Question 39: Error while uninstalling MQ

I'm getting an error while running an uninstall script that gets rid of all MQ packages installed in my system.

When it gets to this step in the script: rpm -e MQSeriesRuntime-U806667-6.0.2-0, I get this error:

ERROR: This maintenance package, "MQSeriesRuntime", is not the most recent maintenance package applied on this system. Please remove the later maintenance package(s) associated with the component "MQSeriesRuntime", before removing this one. Aborting install.

I'm absolutely sureMQSeriesRuntime-U806667-6.0.2-0 is the latest maintenance package on the system. When I "rpm -qa| grep "^MQSeries" I get this:
rpm -qa|grep "^MQSeries"
MQSeriesRuntime-6.0.1-0
MQSeriesRuntime-U806667-6.0.2-0

Everything is gone but these 2 packages. These are the only 2 left on my system but it's telling me there's another one. How do I clear this problem?

A: This should clear it up:

```
rpm -e --nodeps --noscripts MQSeriesRuntime-U806667-
6.0.2-0
rpm -e MQSeriesRuntime ( if this has problems then
add --noscripts)
```

Check that the packages have indeed been removed:

```
rpm -qa | grep MQSeries
```

There may be files left in /opt/mqm, so: rm -rf /opt/mqm/*

Check for symlinks in /usr/bin and /usr/lib that point to (now nonexistent) files in /opt/mqm and remove them.

Question 40: MQ client setup

I am using MQ 5.3 on Windows 2003. I am setting up the MQ client and did the following:
Install MQ client on the client machine.
Created SVRC channel on the server machine where the queue manager is.
Copy the AMQCLCHL.TAB file to the client machine from the server.
Created the env variables on the client.

The things which I am not sure about are:
When I created the new SVRC channel on the server, the AMQCLCHL.TAB didn't get updated and the date stamp was the same.
I am able to put a message to a queue using the client but I don't see the SVRC channel starting.
There is an existing SVRC channel from before for a different client machine, I don't know if this will cause an issue.

The TAB file is not updated and when I tried to view it, I see old information in there but nothing related to the new channel I just created. Are my methods correct?

A: Your method looks right. Client connections are not specific to a given client machine and one client channel can be used by multiple clients.

Make sure you take the TAB file from the @ipcc folder. Early versions of v5.3 put copies in odd places.

To update your tab file, you have to create CLNTCONN channel(s) that correspond to your SVRCONN channel(s). Make sure the CLNTCONN definitions include the connection information (IP, port) for access to your queue manager.

On the server side make sure the MQ listener is running.

Lastly, you forgot to create client connection.

Question 41: AMQ4760

We are currently running on 6.0.1.1 and have been trying to upgrade our MQ systems to 6.0.2.

While installing the refresh pack, I keep getting this error AMQ4760. I have tried installing with amqicsdn MQPINUSEOK=1 option but it did not help.

The error message also points to amqicsdn.txt. What should I look for?

A: If you apply a WebSphere® MQ v5.3 CSD on Windows and the CSD installation fails and you receive message AMQ4760, then do the ff:

The errors that occur during CSD installation are recorded in a file named amqicsdn.txt. This file is located in the user \temp directory. Open this file and search from the bottom upwards for the string "***".

If it shows that there a number of files on the system which are newer than those being installed, then try to rename the target file in E:\MQSeries\bin\amqxcs2.dll (Example: amqxcs2.dll_OLD). Install the CSD.

Question 42: MQ 5.3 CSD 10 issue installing on W2K

I am getting an AMQ4757 while installing CSD10 on Windows 2000. I have stopped all the known services such as:
BGS-SD Service
IBM Config Mgr
IBM MQ Series
Patrol Agent
Symantec Anti Virus Client
Version Control Agent
Windows Management Instrumentation.
WAS
Performance Logs and Alerts.

There are no "amq*" processes running as can be seen in the task manager and there is also no "MQ" icon in the task bar in the bottom right hand corner. What is causing the error?

A: The DLL's are locked by non-MQ processes. To install of a CSD for WebSphere MQ v5.3 for Windows®, follow these steps:

Download the CSD from the web.
Run the install program and note the temporary folder to which the install files are being extracted, something like: C:\Program Files\IBM\Source\WebSphere MQ CSD##EnUs'.
Exit the CSD install process.
Once the CSD file is saved in your work station, extract them to a folder of your choice (for example: C:\CSD).
In C:\CSD folder, you should see many other folders and a couple of files.
Among those files, there should be the amqicsdn.exe file.
Open the Command Prompt window and run the following: amqicsdn MQPINUSEOK=1. This setting allows the install to continue even if we find that files are in use.
The window with the progress indicator of the CSD install should pop up and the CSD installation should complete without being interrupted.

Now, to uninstall a CSD for WebSphere MQ v5.3 for Windows, use the Command Prompt window instead and switch to the latest CSD directory then run the following command:

```
amqicsdn MQPUNINST=1 MQPINUSEOK=1
```

Question 43: MQ6 installation issue on XP

I am trying to install MQ 6 on Windows XP machine and it gives me the following error when I click on Install:

"Error opening installation log file. Verify that the specified log file location exists and is writable";

I went thru the following ini file "MQParms.ini". The default log path was:
"MQPLOG=%temp%\MQParms.txt"

I checked in that path and there was no file. What could be causing the error?

A: Try and do the following:

1. Ensure that the location specified temporary directory is having the write access.

2. Right Click My Computer icon > Properties > Advanced > Environment you will see the temp folder settings there > Click edit then change the folder paths as you want, then try it.

Question 44: Segmentation

In the manual "MQ v 6.0 Fundamentals", chapter "4.6.7" states that:

"Messages that are larger than 100 MB can be broken into smaller segments. Segmentation when sending messages and reassembly of the whole message when receiving messages can be performed manually by an application or automatically by a queue manager"

How can I do that?

A: There are two possible options to follow:

1. Manually divide your message into smaller parts and send it as few messages.

```
Code:
...
MQPutMessageOptions pmo= new MQPutMessageOptions();
pmo.options=MQC.MQPMO_FAIL_IF_QUIESCING |
MQC.MQPMO_SYNCPOINT;

        MQMessage mqmessage=new MQMessage();
mqmessage.format=MQC.MQFMT_STRING;
mqmessage.messageType = MQC.MQMT_REQUEST;
mqmessage.writeString(message1);
mqmessage.messageFlags=MQC.MQMF_SEGMENT;

queue.put(mqmessage, pmo);

        MQMessage mqmessage2=new MQMessage();
mqmessage2.format=MQC.MQFMT_STRING;
mqmessage2.messageType = MQC.MQMT_REQUEST;
mqmessage2.writeString(message2);
mqmessage2.messageFlags=MQC.MQMF_LAST_SEGMENT;

mqmessage2.groupId=mqmessage.groupId;
mqmessage2.messageSequenceNumber=mqmessage.messageSeq
uenceNumber+1;
mqmessage2.offset=message1.length();

queue.put(mqmessage2, pmo);

qMgr.commit();
```

...

2. sk QMGR to divide this message for you :

```
Code:
...
message.messageFlags=MQC.MQMF_SEGMENTATION_ALLOWED;
queue.put(message,pmo);
...
```

Now, you can MQPut () a 125 GB message and Queue Manager will split it into 10 MB chunks and send it over the channel.

On the remote side you will have 10 messages. You can get it one by one or you can ask QMGR to split it for you into one big message and receive entire message by one GET.

```
Code:
...
MQGetMessageOptions gmo = new MQGetMessageOptions();
gmo.options = MQC.MQGMO_FAIL_IF_QUIESCING|
MQC.MQGMO_COMPLETE_MSG;
queueIN.get(retrievemqmessage, gmo);
...
```

Question 45: Two Qmgr with same name

I am trying to setup a channel between two systems. It works fine and we are able to send messages over the transmission queues if the queue managers on the systems are different.

If the channels and queues are created on both the systems where the queue managers on them both are WBRK6_DEFAULT_QUEUE_MANAGER, the channel can successfully ping. But, I cannot put any messages on the remote queue definition, why is this so?

A: If you have two queue managers with the same name, it will confuse the automatic name resolution; the system will be unable to tell which of the 2 queue managers the message is destined for.

You'll need to use explicit transmission queues in the remote queue definitions and/or queue managers aliases to deal with.

Or use recommended best practice and name the queue managers differently. Aside from the problems with name resolution, it makes tracking messages and error resolution harder. There's also very seldom a good reason for having 2 identically named queue managers when you drill through the requirements.

Also, if you ever go to clustering it simply won't work.

Question 46: Starting mq at boot on Linux

How can I start MQ at server boot in Linux/Unix?

A: Create a script that looks like this:

```
Code:
#! /bin/sh
#

# init the rc.status env
. /etc/rc.status

echo "Running Prototype RC for MQSeries "
rc_reset

case "$1" in

start)
        echo -n "Starting WebSphere MQSeries"
        su - mqm -c "cd /opt/mqm/bin; ./strmqm yourqmgr "
        su - mqm -c "cd /opt/mqm/bin; ./strmqcsv yourqmgr "
        su - mqm -c "cd /opt/mqm/bin; ./runmqlsr -m
yourqmgr -t TCP -p 1414 & "
        su - mqm -c "cd /opt/mqm/bin; ./runmqtrm -q
YOUR.INIT.QUEUE -m yourqmgr & "
        rc_status -v
        ;;

stop)
        echo -n "Stoping WebSphere MQSeries"
        su - mqm -c "cd /opt/mqm/bin; ./endmqm -i yourqmgr "
        su - mqm -c "cd /opt/mqm/bin; ./endmqlsr -m
yourqmgr & "

        rc_status -v
        ;;

restart)
        echo -n "Restarting WebSphere MQSeries"
        su - mqm -c "cd /opt/mqm/bin; ./endmqm -i yourqmgr"
        su - mqm -c "cd /opt/mqm/bin; ./endmqlsr -m
yourqmgr& "
        su - mqm -c "cd /opt/mqm/bin; ./strmqm yourqmgr"
        su - mqm -c "cd /opt/mqm/bin; ./strmqcsv yourqmgr"
        su - mqm -c "cd /opt/mqm/bin; ./runmqlsr -m
yourqmgr-t TCP -p 1414 & "
        su - mqm -c "cd /opt/mqm/bin; ./runmqtrm -q
YOUR.INIT.QUEUE -m yourqmgr& "
```

```
        rc_status
        ;;

status)
        echo -n "WebSphere MQSeries status "
        su - mqm -c "cd /opt/mqm/bin; ./dspmq "
        su - mqm -c "cd /opt/mqm/bin; ./dspmqcsv "
        rc_status -v
        ;;

*)
        echo "Usage: $0 { start | stop | restart | status }"
        exit 1
        ;;
esac
rc_exit 0
```

You will need to be root to do this.
Put this file in /etc/rc.d. and call this one mqseries but the name doesn't matter.

Go to /etc/rc.d/rc2.d and create 2 links to this file.
K20mqseries -> ../mqseries
S20mqseries -> ../mqseries

The number, for example 20 can be any number that is not already assigned in this directory. The Sxxmqseries gets called when Linux boots up in ring 2 and Sxxmqseries gets called when Linux shuts down.

Repeat this for each ring you want to start/stop MQ, i.e. rc3.d, rc4.d, etc

Question 47: Unable to start MQIPT service

We are using an MQ IPT in our production environment. Now I carry the responsibility of recreating it in a different environment. I installed the IPT and modified the mqipt.conf file. I added the MQ-IPT as a windows service using the command mqiptservice install path. When I try to start the MQIPT in the services window, the following error is generated:

Error:1067
Event log: The description for Event ID (0) in Source (MQInternetPassThru) cannot be found. The local computer may not have the necessary registry information or message DLL files to display messages from a remote computer. You may be able to use the /AUXSOURCE= flag to retrieve this description; see Help and Support for details. The following information is part of the event: MQInternetPassThru error: 1063, StartServiceCtrlDispatcher failed.

Did I miss a step?

A: Do the following if you think you are messing with the system environment:

Set the MQIPT Service to MANUAL startup.
Reboot to ensure you have a clean environment.
Check that the mods for the jvm path are correct, if not, do necessary corrections.
Start the service manually via the services.msc panel.
Check the system event log for errors. Also check the mqipt logs as well.

This will allow you to verify that any changes you have made to the environment are truly correct.

Once you have the IPT service running, don't forget to save the changes you have made in case the system goes belly up and you have to move to another box.

MQIPT is a great support pack but you just have to be careful in how you set it up when running as a service.

Question 48: Refresh Pack 6.0.2.0

I was working with an SA last night on a V6 install on HP and we tried to apply the 6.0.2.0 immediately after the install and it failed. The checkinstall script said that there was a queue manager running so it couldn't continue with the fix pack. This was a new install on a new server so there isn't any way there was a queue manager running as we had just installed the software. I searched for amq processes and semaphores and memory segments and didn't find any as expected.

How can I successfully install the refresh pack?

A: Definitely you will get this issue. Do the following steps to make it work:

Go to /opt/mqm/bin.
Create a symbolic link to amqiclen to /usr/bin/true.
Then install the RP.

Question 49: Symbolic link

I am trying to install CSD12 on MQ manager 5.3 and I am getting an error saying that "Failed to clean System V IPC resources". I have to go through some steps as advised by IBM in order to solve this error. The IBM site says that I must create a symbolic link to /usr/bin/true and then rename amqiclen.

What does it mean to create a symbolic link to /usr/bin/true?

A: Do the following steps:

Copy the amqiclen , use cp -p option.
ln -s /usr/bin/true /opt/mqm/bin/amqiclen.
Start installing.

Note: amqiclen file has to be removed before converting it to a link to /usr/bin/true.
After the installation it will automatically go off.

A symlink is a UNIX construct, a fake directory that points to another location. It is like a Windows shortcut but far more sophisticated & useful. It is created with the "ln" command.

A symbolic link is a file that contains the real path to a file. Think of it as an alias to the real path to a file.

Question 50: 64-bit install issue

I am trying to install MQ6.0 on AIX 5.3. I uninstalled the old version 5.3 and then installed the MQ6.0 and then 6.0.2.0. but I am able to see the dspmqver with only root where as not with mqm userid. It is giving some errors.
dspmqver
exec(): 0509-036 Cannot load program dspmqver because of the following errors:
0509-150 Dependent module /usr/lib/libmqmcs_r.a(shr.o) could not be loaded.
0509-103 The module has an invalid magic number.

A: This is 64-bit versus a 32-bit library issue. The system picks 32 bit MQ libraries when it should select the 64 bit libs.

Most likely the $LIBPATH or $LD_LIBRARY_PATH has (AIX®)/usr/lib or (Sun, HP, Linux)/opt/lib in it. And /[usr| opt]/lib has libmqm* files linked to /[usr|opt]/mqm/lib/* files.

You should edit the LIBPATH or $LD_LIBRARY_PATH to remove the /usr/lib or /opt/lib.

Or add /[usr|opt]/mqm/lib64 to the front of the $LIBPATH or $LD_LIBRARY_PATH
export $LIBPATH=/usr/mqm/lib64:$LIBPATH to add on AIX system.

Question 51: MQ triggering property

I configured queue property as follows:

> Trigger Control : On
> Trigger type : Depth
> Trigger Depth : 5
> Trigger Message Priority:1
> TriggerData:
> Initiation Queue: INITIATION.QUEUE
> Process Name: Process

After trigger executing once, the trigger control is getting off automatically. The case is different if I use Every|First trigger type. What is the reason behind this?

A: This is working as designed. When the event fires and you open the queue the trigger is turned off because you already have the queue open for reading. When your application finishes and has read all messages the triggering needs to be turned on using MQSET and then wait for the next 5 messages.

Question 52: Error during MQ 5.3 install on XP

I am trying to install MQ Server version 5.3 on WinXP Pro SP2 but I always get the following error:

"One or more problem occurred. Review the MSI log file for details (AMQ4739)".

The first error appeared in the log file:

```
MSI (c) (18:54) [14:40:40:499]: Leaked MSIHANDLE
(21) of type 790550 for thread     3968
MSI (c) (18:54) [14:40:40:499]: Leaked MSIHANDLE
(20) of type 790541 for thread 3968
MSI (c) (18:54) [14:40:40:499]: Note: 1: 2769 2:
iwiInstallInitPri 3: 15
DEBUG: Error 2769: Custom Action
iwiInstallInitPri did not close 15 MSIHANDLEs.
Internal Error 2769. iwiInstallInitPri, 15
Action ended 14:40:40: iwiInstallInitPri. Return
value 1.
MSI (c) (18:80) [14:40:40:499]: Doing action:
amqispsn.exe
Action 14:40:40: amqispsn.exe.
```

and then:

```
        1: 14:42:29 MQCA iwiCheckSourceAvailable
info: D:\distr\dev\IBM\WS\CD1-
1\win\WAS\messaging\server\MQSeries\Msi\program
files\IBM\WebSphere MQ\bin\amqicsdn.exe
        1: 14:42:29 MQCA iwiCheckSourceAvailable
info: Component 'Server_base' Installed: 2
Action: 3
        1: 14:42:29 MQCA iwiCheckSourceAvailable
info: This component has no key file specified.
        1: 14:42:29 MQCA iwiCheckSourceAvailable
info: Component 'GuiAdmin_base' Installed: 2
Action: 3
        1: 14:42:29 MQCA iwiCheckSourceAvailable
info: This component has no key file specified.
        1: 14:42:29 MQCA iwiCheckSourceAvailable
info: Component 'MQSeriesServices' Installed: 2
Action: 3
```

```
        1: 14:42:29 MQCA iwiCheckSourceAvailable
info: =============|||| Error, failure, problem,
warning ||||=============
        1: 14:42:29 MQCA iwiCheckSourceAvailable
info: vvvv vvvv
        1: 14:42:29 MQCA iwiCheckSourceAvailable
info: ***Key file not found in source:
        1: 14:42:29 MQCA iwiCheckSourceAvailable
info: D:\distr\dev\IBM\WS\CD1-
1\win\WAS\messaging\server\MQSeries\Msi\program
files\IBM\WebSphere MQ\bin\amqsvc.exe
        1: 14:42:29 MQCA iwiCheckSourceAvailable
info: Component 'MQSeries.msc_en_us' Installed:
2 Action: 3
        1: 14:42:29 MQCA iwiCheckSourceAvailable
info: =============|||| Error, failure, problem,
warning ||||=============
        1: 14:42:29 MQCA iwiCheckSourceAvailable
info: vvvv vvvv
        1: 14:42:29 MQCA iwiCheckSourceAvailable
info: ***Key file not found in source:
```

What could be the cause of the problem?

A: It seems that the MSI installer is the problem. Try to do one of the following:
1. Kill the MSI installer process from the task manager and restart the MSI service.
2. Update the MSI installer from Microsoft and reboot the computer.

Question 53: MQ Backout count

Can I set the MQMD back out count to a specific number and access that MQMD back out count number in another message flow or another queue?

A: Yes. Set the "Back out Threshold" to the count you want to reach. Then set the Back out Retry Queue to the queue that you want or the queue that is being read by the flow you want.

Then, code your original WMB/WBIMB/WMQI/MQSI (hint!) flow to throw errors until the message is backed out.

The message will have a backout count of zero by the time it gets put to the queue identified in the Backout Requeue name since the broker's MQInput node will do an MQPUT to requeue the message. The backout count is an output field for the MQGET call. It is ignored for the MQPUT and MQPUT1 calls. The initial value of this field in a message put/requeued with MQPUT/MQPUT1 is 0.

Question 54: MQ Explorer Access limitation

We are planning the MQ security authorization in our organization. Our problem is MQ explorer has been installed on various developers desktop from where they can connect to the Broker Queue manager for message testing. We want to put access authorization to the entire non-admin user.

Is there any way we can limit the access authority through MQ Explorer? Can I put "read only" security for the SYSTEM.ADMIN.SVRCONN channel and will the developer be able to see the messages?

A: You can put a mcauser with "inq" and "disp" only authority on the channel. You need to give him put authority for the SYSTEM.COMMAND.QUEUE and GET authority for the SYSTEM.MQEXPLORER.MODEL queue (names to be checked against your installation).

Create a different channel for the administrators.

Question 55: MQ Explorer to control remote Queues

How can I see and control the Q Managers created in MQ v5.3(Solaris m/c) from Windows through MQ Explorer?

A: To manually create a new connection from WebSphere MQ Explorer to a remote queue manager:

In the Navigator view, right-click the Queue Managers folder, then click Show/Hide Queue Managers. The Show/Hide Queue Managers dialog opens.

Click Add... The Add Queue Manager dialog opens.
In the Queue manager name field, type the name of the queue manager to which you want to connect.
Ensure that Connect directly is selected, and then click Next.
Ensure that Specify connection details are selected and then type the following details: In the Host name or IP address field, type the name of the computer that hosts the remote queue manager; Use one of the following formats:

The short hostname, for example, andrea. The remote computer must be in the same domain as your local computer. The fully qualified hostname, for example, andrea.nicole.ibm.com can be used this if the remote computer is in a different domain to your local computer.

The IP address, for example 9.20.1.156
In the Port number field, type the port number; for example, 1416

Optional: Select the Autoreconnect check box to configure WebSphere MQ Explorer to automatically reconnect to the queue manager if the connection is lost.

Optional: Change the frequency with which WebSphere MQ Explorer refreshes its information about the queue manager. To prevent WebSphere MQ Explorer automatically refreshing its information about the queue manager, click No queue manager refresh interval; to specify a different refresh interval, click

Specify queue manager refresh interval, then type the number of seconds that you want WebSphere MQ Explorer to wait before refreshing its information about the queue manager. Click Finish.

Question 56: Integrating Websphere MQ w/ Jboss

How do I integrate WebSphere MQ with Jboss application server?

A: With the release of IBM WebSphereMQ 6.0.2.1, IBM has provided a JCA 1.5 compliant resource adapter enabling integration with WebSphere MQ Series from any J2EE 1.4 compliant application server without the use of proprietary or custom integration code. This page details the process of deploying the IBM resource adapter for inbound and outbound JMS connectivity. The resource adapter supports connectivity to both WebSphereMQ version 6.0 and 5.3 (Client mode only).

Use of distributed transactions (XA) with the JMS resource adapter for both outbound and inbound connectivity requires the deployment of the Extended Transaction Client.

Deploy the IBM JMS resource adapter: The IBM JMS resource adapter can be found in the following location from the WebSphereMQ 6.0.2.1 distribution:

`MQ_HOME/Java/lib/jca/wmq.jmsra.rar`

where MQ_HOME is the root of your IBM WebSphereMQ installation directory. Copy the wmq.jmsra.rar file to the deploy directory of your JBoss distribution to deploy the resource adapter.

If you will be migrating from an existing IBM WebSphere MQ installation on JBoss, the following IBM WebSphereMQ jar files should be removed:

`com.ibm.mq.jar`
`com.ibm.mqjms.jar`
`dhbcore.jar`

These files are now provided by the IBM JMS resource adapter and must be removed to avoid versioning conflicts. A deployment error with code MQJCA1008 indicates this condition.

Create the WebSphereMQ Administrative Object(s): Prior to the release of the WebSphere MQ JMS resource adapter, destinations hosted by WebSphereMQ either had to be bound manually into JNDI or accessed via the WebSphereMQ IntialContext against the MQ host. The correct way to configure and manage destination objects using the JMS resource adapter is through the AdminObject facility provided by JCA 1.5. The following shows how this is accomplished via a standard JMX service deployment:

```
<server>
    <mbean
code="org.jboss.resource.deployment.AdminObject"
name="jboss.jca:service=WASDestination,name=QueueName
">
        <depends optional-attribute-
name="RARName">jboss.jca:service=RARDeployment,name='
wmq.jmsra.rar'</depends>
<attribute name="JNDIName">JNDI_NAME</attribute>
        <attribute
name="Type">javax.jms.Queue</attribute>
        <attribute name="Properties">
baseQueueManagerName=QM_NAME
            baseQueueName=BASE_QUEUE_NAME
        </attribute>
    </mbean>
</server>
```

Placing this file into the JBoss deployment directory will create and bind a javax.jms.Queue destination into the JBoss JNDI tree. The QM_NAME and BASE_QUEUE_NAME should be replaced with values in your environment. The JNDI name can be anything, but it is generally a good practice to conform to standard naming conventions (i.e. queue/SomeQueuName).

Configure an MDB listening on a destination in WebSphereMQ:

The MDB configuration:

```
<enterprise-beans>
        <message-driven>
            <ejb-name>TestMDB</ejb-name>
```

```
        <ejb-
class>org.jboss.test.TestListener</ejb-class>
        <messaging-
type>javax.jms.MessageListener</messaging-type>
        <transaction-type>Container</transaction-
type>
        <activation-config>
            <activation-config-property>
                <activation-config-property-
name>destination</activation-config-property-name>
                <activation-config-property-
value>DESTINATION_NAME</activation-config-property-
value>
            </activation-config-property>
            <activation-config-property>
                <activation-config-property-
name>destinationType</activation-config-property-
name>
                <activation-config-property-
value>DESTINATION_TYPE</activation-config-property-
value>
            </activation-config-property>
            <activation-config-property>
                <activation-config-property-
name>useJNDI</activation-config-property-name>
                <activation-config-property-
value>false</activation-config-property-value>
            </activation-config-property>
            <activation-config-property>
                <activation-config-property-
name>hostName</activation-config-property-name>
                <activation-config-property-
value>MQ_HOST_NAME</activation-config-property-value>
            </activation-config-property>
            <activation-config-property>
                <activation-config-property-
name>queueManager</activation-config-property-name>
                <activation-config-property-
value>QUEUE_MANAGER_NAME</activation-config-property-
value>
            </activation-config-property>
        </activation-config>
    </message-driven>
</enterprise-beans>
```

While most of the above properties are self explanatory, notice
the property:

```
<activation-config-property>
        <activation-config-property-
name>useJNDI</activation-config-property-name>
          <activation-config-property-
value>false</activation-config-property-value>
    </activation-config-property>
```

By default (false), the JMS resource adapter will interpret the
destination name as a Queue or Topic configured on
WebSphereMQ. Setting this value to true will force the JMS
resource adapter to acquire the JMS destination from the
application server's JNDI namespace. Destinations can be bound
into JNDI via the aforementioned administrative object facility
described above.

Finally, the jboss.xml descriptor:

```
<jboss>
    <enterprise-beans>
        <message-driven>
            <resource-adapter-
name>wmq.jmsra.rar</resource-adapter-name>
            <ejb-name>TestMDB</ejb-name>
            <configuration-name>Standard Message
Inflow Driven Bean</configuration-name>
        </message-driven>
    </enterprise-beans>
</jboss>
```

WARNING: The above configuration uses standard jca inflow. If
you are going to create your own configurations or invoker-
proxy-bindings DO NOT use the JMS specific invoker proxy. The
WSMQ resource adapter does not support all the standard
properties; in particular it does not support acknowledgeMode or
subscriptionDurability.

Configure a JMS connection factory: Configuration of a JMS
connection factory is trivial using the standard ds.xml file
mechanism:

```
<tx-connection-factory>
```

```
<jndi-name>JNDI_NAME</jndi-name>
<xa-transaction/>
<rar-name>wmq.jmsra.rar</rar-name>
<connection-
definition>javax.jms.ConnectionFactory</connection-
definition>
       <config-property name="hostName"
type="java.lang.String">QUEUE_MANAGER_HOST</config-
property>
       <config-property name="queueManager"
type="java.lang.String">QUEUE_MANAGER_NAME</config-
property>
       <max-pool-size>20</max-pool-size>
  </tx-connection-factory>
```

Question 57: MQJMS1025: failed to browse message

I have WAS 6.0.2.17 and using MQ 5.3 (csd10). JMS Resources have been defined in WAS console using JMS Provider ->WebSphere MQ. The WAS variable MQ_INSTALL_ROOT and MQJMS_LIB_ROOT point to MQ 5.3.

I get the following error when the application starts up:

```
[4/26/07 18:47:15:390 EDT] 00000038 ConnectionEve A
J2CA0056I: The Connection Manager received a fatal
connection error from the Resource Adaptor for
resource jms/wFactory. The exception which was
received is javax.jms.JMSException: MQJMS1025: failed
to browse message
[4/26/07 18:47:15:485 EDT] 00000038 JMSExceptionL E
WMSG0018E: Error on JMSConnection for MDB exMDBean,
JMSDestination queue/wQueue: javax.jms.JMSException:
MQJMS1025: failed to browse message at
com.ibm.mq.jms.services.ConfigEnvironment.newExceptio
n (ConfigEnvironment.java:553) at
com.ibm.mq.jms.MQQueueAgentThread1Impl.browse
(MQQueueAgentThread1Impl.java:441) at
com.ibm.mq.jms.MQQueueAgentThread.run
(MQQueueAgentThread.java:1623) at
java.lang.Thread.run (Thread.java:534)
---- Begin backtrace for Nested Throwables
com.ibm.mq.MQException: MQJE001: Completion Code 2,
Reason 2016 at
com.ibm.mq.jms.MQQueueAgentThread1Impl.browseMsg
(MQQueueAgentThread1Impl.java:554) at
com.ibm.mq.jms.MQQueueAgentThread1Impl.browse
(MQQueueAgentThread1Impl.java:318)at
com.ibm.mq.jms.MQQueueAgentThread.run
(MQQueueAgentThread.java:1623) at
java.lang.Thread.run(Thread.java:534)
```

A: The "mqrc" is a very useful command. It decodes MQ Reason Codes such as the one in the MQException you've encountered.

In this case we get:

```
mqrc 2016

2016 0x000007e0 MQRC_GET_INHIBITED

    mqrc 2016

    2016 0x000007e0 MQRC_GET_INHIBITED
```

It appears that your queue has its GET attribute set to DISABLED. If you want to get messages from it (including browsing), it needs to have its GET attribute set to ENABLED. You can do this with an mqsc command such as:

```
ALTER QLOCAL('queue.name') GET(ENABLED) or with the
MQ Explorer GUI
```

Question 58: Secondary log files

Secondary Log Files are needed when the Primary Log Files are filled as I understood from Documentation.

In Circular Logging, there is no way that primary logs will get filled as it is circular. If so, why would we need secondary log Files in Circular logging?

A: The number and size of logfiles determines the logspace.

The size and type (circular/linear) of the logfiles is set at qmgr creation. The number is set at qmgr startup (i.e. can be changed to allow for more logspace).

If more logspace than what has been specified for primary logspace is needed the qmgr will create secondary logfiles up to the number specified at startup. If this is still not sufficient you might see things like rolling back long lived transaction in the log.

In circular logging, it is quite obvious which the secondary log files are. It is much less obvious in linear logging unless you have just run rcdmqimg and archived the old logs.

The qmgr manages all that transparently. The only thing you need to do is determine what the maximum logspace is and set it up right.

Question 59: Mirroring messages from multi queues

I am trying to mirror messages coming to two different queues. Each has a name list defined to mirror messages to a different queue. The following are the two entries from qm.ini:

```
ApiExitLocal:
Name=mirrorq1
Function=EntryPoint
Module=/var/mqm/exits/mirrorq
Data=MIRRORQ.NL1
Sequence=11

ApiExitLocal:
Name=mirrorq2
Function=EntryPoint
Module=/var/mqm/exits/mirrorq22
Data=MIRRORQ.NL2
Sequence=12

The following modules exist under /var/mqm/exits

mirrorq
mirrorq_r
mirrorq22
mirrorq22_r
```

This set up works just fine as I wanted. Is there a better way to use one module instead of two as in this case? Also, is it possible to have one ApiExitLocal stanza with different names?

A: Your namelist can specify more than set of {sourceQ,targetQ,targetQmgr} but only up to the maxlength of the namelist.

You can modify the exit, given that it's sample code, and change it to read it's configuration from anywhere it wants, or to accept a LIST of namelists in the "Data option".

Specifying multiple source and target queues in the name list can simplify your approach.

Question 60: MQ Java Triggered server example

I am using Java API for MQ for working with queue. How can we set triggering on that application?

A: Try the following example:

```
Code:
import java.io.*;
import java.lang.*;
import com.ibm.mq.*;

class MQTrigger
{

    private String structId;
    private String version;
    private String qName;
    private String processName;
    private String triggerData;
    private String applType;
    private String applId;
    private String envData;
    private String userData;
    private String qMgrName;

    /******************************************************
*****/
    /* Constructor to parse the TMC stucture and set
*/
    /* the class attributes.
*/
    /* Values derived from cmqc.h
*/
    /******************************************************
*****/
    public MQTrigger(String tmcStruct) throws
StringIndexOutOfBoundsException
    {

        structId    = tmcStruct.substring(0,3).trim();
        version     = tmcStruct.substring(4,8).trim();
        qName       = tmcStruct.substring(8,55).trim();
```

```
        processName =
tmcStruct.substring(56,103).trim();
        triggerData =
tmcStruct.substring(104,167).trim();
        applType    =
tmcStruct.substring(168,171).trim();
        applId      =
tmcStruct.substring(172,427).trim();
        envData     =
tmcStruct.substring(428,555).trim();
        userData    =
tmcStruct.substring(556,683).trim();

        /*************************************************
**/
        /* A TMC version 2 structure includes the
*/
        /* queue mananger name which is not present in
*/
        /* a version 1 structure
*/
        /*************************************************
**/
        if (version.compareTo(new String("2")) == 0)
        {
            qMgrName =
tmcStruct.substring(684,730).trim();
}
        else
        {
            qMgrName = "";
        }
    }
    public String getStructId()
    {
        return(structId);
    }
    public String getVersion()
    {
        return(version);
    }
    public String getQueueName()
    {
        return(qName);
    }
    public String getProcessName()
    {
        return(processName);
    }
```

```
   public String getTriggerData()
   {
      return(triggerData);
   }
   public String getApplicationType()
   {
      return(applType);
   }
   public String getApplicationId()
   {
      return(applId);
   }
   public String getEnvironmentData()
   {
      return(envData);
   }
   public String getUserData()
   {
      return(userData);
   }
   public String getQueueManagerName()
   {
      return(qMgrName);
   }
};
public class JavaTrigger
{
   private MQQueueManager qMgr;

   public static void main (String args[]) throws
IOException
   {
      if (args.length < 1)
      {
         System.out.println("This must be a triggered
application");
}
      else
      {
         System.out.println("MQGet: browse and
optionally get messages");
         JavaTrigger jt = new JavaTrigger();
         jt.start(args);
      }
      System.exit(0);
   }


   public void start(String args[])
```

```
    {
        try
        {

            /********************************************
********/
            /* Create a MQTrigger class object to read
the TMC    */
            /* structure into the correct attribute.
*/
            /********************************************
********/
            MQTrigger tmc = new MQTrigger(args[0]);


            /**********************************************
***********/
            /* Connect to the queue manager identified
by the     */
            /* trigger.
*/
            /**********************************************
***********/

            qMgr = new
MQQueueManager(tmc.getQueueManagerName());

            /********************************************
********/
            /* Open the queue identified by the trigger.
*/
            /********************************************
********/

            int openOptions = MQC.MQOO_INPUT_AS_Q_DEF |
MQC.MQOO_FAIL_IF_QUIESCING;

            MQQueue triggerQueue =
qMgr.accessQueue(tmc.getQueueName(),
                                                open
Options,
                                                null
, null, null);
            /********************************************
********/
            /* Set up our options to get the first
message        */
```

```
          /* Wait 5 seconds to be cetain all messages
are       */
          /* processed.
*/
          /************************************************
********/
          MQGetMessageOptions gmo = new
MQGetMessageOptions();
          gmo.options = MQC.MQGMO_WAIT |
MQC.MQGMO_CONVERT;
          gmo.waitInterval = 5000;

          MQMessage triggerMessage = new MQMessage();

          /************************************************
********/
          /* Read each message from the queue until
there are  */
          /* no more messages to get.
*/
          /************************************************
********/
long rc = 0;
          do
          {
             rc = 0;
             try
             {
                /************************************
**********/
                /* Set the messageId and correlationId
to none */
                /* to get all messages with no message
*/
                /* selection.
*/
                /************************************
**********/
                triggerMessage.clearMessage();
                triggerMessage.correlationId =
MQC.MQCI_NONE;
                triggerMessage.messageId =
MQC.MQMI_NONE;

                triggerQueue.get(triggerMessage, gmo);
                String msg =
triggerMessage.readString(triggerMessage.getMessageLe
ngth());
```

```
              /*****************************************
**********/
              /* Insert business logic for the
message here. */
              /* For this sample, echo the message
*/
              /*****************************************
*********/
              System.out.println("Message: " + msg);

          }
          catch (MQException mqEx)
          {
              rc = mqEx.reasonCode;
              if (rc !=
MQException.MQRC_NO_MSG_AVAILABLE)
              {
                  System.out.println("Get Message
failed with rc = "
                                        + rc);
              }
          }
          catch (Exception ex)
          {
              System.out.println("Generic exception:
" + ex);
              rc = 1;
          }
      } while (rc == 0);

      /***********************************************
*******/
      /* Cleanup MQ resources prior to exiting.
*/
      /***********************************************
*******/
      triggerQueue.close();
      qMgr.disconnect();
  }
  catch (MQException mqEx)
  {
      System.out.println("MQ failed with
completion code = "
                          + mqEx.completionCode
                          + " and reason code = " +
mqEx.reasonCode);
      }
    }
}
```

Question 61: MQ CSD2 installation

I am trying to install CSD 2 for MQ 6. I am getting the "files already in use" error. I tried this code: "WebSphereMQMDV6.0.2.0EnUs.exe -a MQPINUSEOK=1" but still got an error of: "IBM Websphere MQ files are in use. Stop activity and retry (AMQ47570)"

I am sure I don't have any amq processes running. Is there a workaround for this problem?

A: Here is one possible workaround:

Extract the CSD into a directory known to you.
Set the above variable using set MQPINUSEOK=1.
Use amqicsdn to start the installation.

Another option is to run "listdlls" to check the dlls in use on the system. Collect the output into a file and search the file for MQ. End any applications with MQ dlls loaded.

You may need to end all java apps. Maybe all jars on the CLASSPATH are loaded into every Java app at startup, so if this includes any WMQ jars then they will be in use.

Question 62: File system status during v5.3 - v6 upgrade

Current setup: AIX with WMQ v5.3 csd11, HA managed by Veritas

WMQ executables are in /usr/mqm on each LPAR; data and log files in /var/mqm and /var/mqm/log are mounted by Veritas when the queue manager is brought up.

Our plan for migration to v6 is to move queue manager to LPAR B, uninstall v5.3 and install v6 on LPAR A. Then, move queue manager to LPAR A and repeat the upgrade steps on LPAR B.

I know that the first time the queue manager is brought up under v6, I should use "strmqm -c" and NOT start a listener. No problem there.

The AIX Quick Beginnings guide makes me wonder if /var/mqm and /var/mqm/log need to be mounted on LPAR A during the installation of v6. Are there any files there that get touched during the installation itself? Will we be safe to have them offline until the time the queue manager is to be brought up?

A: The installation will create and initialize the /var/mqm directory structure if it does not exist and set correct ownership and permissions if it does.

Question 63: Migrating SSL certificates manual section

The migration manual has lengthy detailed section on the topic of SSL certificate migration. The lead-in paragraph contains this text:

WebSphere MQ Version 6.0 provides the Global Security Toolkit (GSKit) on Windows platforms for improved SSL (Secure Sockets Layer) support for queue manager and WebSphere MQ client channels. Follow the guidance in this section to determine whether WebSphere MQ Version 5.3 queue managers or clients have been set up to use SSL connections, and to ensure these channels continue to work with WebSphere MQ Version 6.0. The migration process causes a copy of the certificates stored in the WebSphere MQ Certificate Stores used by WebSphere MQ Version 5.3, to be migrated to a GSKit Key database.

Does this section of the Migration Manual address Windows only?

A: Yes, that section of the Migration Manual addresses Windows only.

WMQ V5.3 for Windows used Microsoft certificate stores for certificate management and WMQ V6.0 for Windows uses GSKit. This change in underlying certificate management application brings Windows in line with UNIX and leads to a few migration considerations, as described in the manual. Other platforms did not change their certificate management application.

Question 64: MQ Infrastructure and SOX compliance

I think that MQSeries Infrastructure SOX compliance should consist of eliminating clear channels and having an effective authentication scheme. I worked on a project where authentication was provided (via one-way SSL/self-signed certificates) with channel exits. The client-side exits provided the user-ID and password and the server-side exit authenticated the user-ID/password via LDAP.

Could authentication have been provided satisfactorily without the security exits had two-way SSL (with client authentication) been implemented?

A: If you need to authenticate the actual user, you need a client exit.

You can create role-based security without an exit by setting an MCA user on client channels, and giving each individual their own cert. Then the cert ensures that the user is trusted, and allowed to connect to the channel, and the MCA User ensures that anyone who is allowed to connect to the channel can only do certain things.

Then your only problem is controlling access to the certificates.

You should make sure to control access to the production environments at the network level using a real firewall. Strongly consider disallowing any direct connection from any personal desktop machines and require all access through an authenticating proxy or a shared console machine.

Question 65: JCE file not found error while running gsk7ikm

When I run the gsk7ikm I got the following error: "The Java Cryptographic Extension (JCE) was not found. Please check that the JCE files have been installed in correct directory"

When I checked, the jce files <java-home>\lib\security and necessary files are installed there. Also, I have defined the variable java_home to indicate <java_install> directory.

What could have caused this problem?

A: You need to use the <mq-install>/gskit/jre/.

Clustering: Issues on Websphere MQ Clustering

Question 66: Mixed 5.3 and 6.0 FRs during staged migration

I plan on migrating MQ5.3 cluster on AIX (about 8 servers). To avoid application outage, we are migrating half of the servers first with 1 FR included then the other half at a later date. Are there any issues of having one 5.3 FR and another 6.0 FR in the same cluster?

A: Due to the current layout of the apps the current FRs cannot be migrated in the same window. What we'll do is promote one of the members of the first batch to be another FR and demote the FR from the other batch to PR. That way all FRs will be migrated first.

Question 67: Connection between client & QM in a cluster

I want to make a connection between a client (which is on a WIN server) and QMgrs (V 5.3 on UNIX), which are located in a cluster. I have two QMgrs, QM1 and QM2. On each QMgrs, I have the same instance of the Queue QLC. The clients have to poll these queues to get messages but I can't do that with the variable MQSERVER because I can just define 1 QMgrs. Can I do this?

A: All clients only connect to a single queue manager; clustering doesn't change that. Hence, to service both queues you need 2 instances for your application.

The reason behind this is that clusters are designed for workload balancing, splitting the inbound messages between 1-n queue managers, typically sited on different machines to spread the resource load. There's no point to this if you then read all the messages with a single application instance; you might just as well save some time/resource & use a single queue manager.

Question 68: Publish/Subscribe not working

In Broker Toolkit, I have created several topics to subscribe to (e.g. Test). I am using RFHUtilc.exe to test pub/sub. To start the utility, I have created a batch file with the following:

```
set MQSERVER=<channel name>/TCP/<server ip
address>(1414)
set PATH=C:\opt\rfhutil - ih03;%PATH%
set PATH=C:\opt\rfhutil;%PATH%
start rfhutilc.exe
```

After opening up the utility with this batch file, I enter the queue manager name WBRK6_DEFAULT_QUEUE_MANAGER in the Queue Manager Name (to connect to) field under the Main tab. I click on the PubSub tab, and select Sub from the Request Type. I enter the Topic "Test/#", and PUB.SEND in the Subscription Queue field. (PUB.SEND is a queue on the queue manager WBRK6_DEFAULT_QUEUE_MANAGER). I select the queue manager from the drop down Queue Manager to Connect To menu, and then hit the "Write Message" button. The broker/configuration manager, and queue managers are running.

When I go to the Broker toolkit and query subscriptions, I do not see anything in the list. Am I missing a step or process?

A: Yes, you are missing a big step. Make sure your broker is at least 6.0.0.3

Make your subscribe messages request messages and specify a reply to qmgr and reply to queue, on the pub/sub tab ask for full feedback.

Now when you send the subscription message you will get a feedback message (pscr). This will tell you if /why the subscription may have failed.

Before level 6.0.0.3 we had a lot of authorization problems. On pub/sub especially if RFHutil was not connected directly to the broker.

Question 69: Cluster alias queue

An application writes a message to a cluster alias queue. This cluster alias points to a local queue that lives on a partial member. If that partial member is unavailable (e.g. system crash) where do the messages end up?

A: It depends if there are other valid targets like another clustered queue to which the messages could be delivered. If there are, it will go there and if not, it will sit in the cluster xmitq until it can be delivered.

One of the benefits of using clustering is it allows an architecture which prevents the situation you're describing.

Question 70: Queue Manager is a full/partial repository

Can I tell that this particular qmgr is holding a full or partial repository if I am not aware of the other qmgrs in the same cluster?

What attribute(s) differentiate between a full & partial repository?

A: Check the display clusqmgr command - qmtype attribute should tell you what you want to know. This is the easiest and fastest way to find out where the repositories are in a cluster. You only need to be connected to a qmgr on the cluster (doesn't matter whether full or partial), thus: "dis clusqmgr(*) qmtype where (qmtype eq repos)" will give you a list of the repositories.

Also, you can set QMGR as full repository by:

```
Code:
ALTER QMGR REPOS(CLUSTER_NAME)
```

So if this parameter of QMGR is not empty it is full repository.

Do not forget the REPOSNL attribute. So a QMGR can be full repository even if the REPOS attribute is empty. To check if QMGR is full repository you have to check REPOS and REPOSNL attribute. If one of them is not empty QMGR is full repository.

Question 71: Interconnected cluster

I currently have a cluster with two full repository QMs and three partials. I'm considering adding a second cluster to the same QMs but I'm not sure if I need to. The existing cluster handles OLTP type work. The new cluster would handle more batch-like work. What are the things should I consider when making this sort of decision?

A: You should not design MQ clustering based on any application criteria at all other than the basic need to load-balance work between instances of the same application.

Many are against overlapped clusters and multiple clusters where one will do just fine. Most of this comes out because of an understanding that clustering was designed to do two things, provide simplified administration and provide workload balancing. Disasters occurred when people went way overboard and designed for application specific clusters and overlapped everything.

Also, it seems to me that the MQ network should be designed and managed by the MQ administrators, based on physical network and administrative requirements, rather than by MQ developers based on application requirements.

Designing means understanding your applications, data, current- and future-workloads, hardware capacity, and more importantly, service-level agreements.

None of these really has anything directly to do with MQ clusters. MQ clusters allow multiple instances of an application to process your work (OLTP and batch).

If all server hardware is at maximum capacity (RAM, disk, cpu, telecom), then any new OLTP and/or batch will/might be a problem for you. Add more (hardware) - another processor with MQ, for example, might save OLTP and batch.

Just to be on the safe side, make sure that OLTP and batch traffic have different priorities. OLTP traffic should have a higher priority than Batch traffic in any case.

Using different priorities will improve your response time during the batch transmission.

Imagine a batch process where you dump thousands of messages into a queue that is load balanced in the cluster. Any request coming in and going to the same qmgr as the batch will have to wait behind those in the xmitq. If the priorities are higher for online than batch (remember the default for cluster xmitq is priority), the online messages will move to the head of the queue and not have to wait until the batch is transferred.

Of course this comes with a slight performance impact but still way less than if the message had to wait in the xmitq until the batch has been transferred.

Question 72: Cluster setup - channel not starting

I have defined a simple cluster with 2 QM's on Windows XP:

QM1 listening on port 1414
QM2 listening on port 1415

CLUSSDR on QM2 starts without errors and corresponding CLUSRCVR on QM1 starts fine.

CLUSSDR channel on QM1 doesn't starts and goes to retry mode. I tried to ping the channel, I am getting reason code 2195 (AMQ4048). In the QM1 error log I see "'TO.QM2' on the remote machine is not of a suitable type" . TO.QM2 on QM2 is defined as CLUSRCVR.

I have defined the channels:
QM1: DEFINE CHANNEL(TO.QM2) CHLTYPE(CLUSSDR) TRPTYPE(TCP)
 CONNAME('MachineName(1415)') CLUSTER(TEST)
QM2:DEFINE CHANNEL(TO.QM2) CHLTYPE(CLUSRCVR) TRPTYPE(TCP)
 CONNAME(MachineName)

What is causing those errors?

A: Assuming that you have a listener running on QM2 on port 1415:

Your receiver channel is not setup right, it should be:

```
Code:
def chl(to.qm2) chltype(clusrcvr) trptype(tcp) +
conname('MachineName(1415)') cluster(test)
```

With your definition, the default port of 1414 is assumed and the channel type does not match for an automatic cluster definition.

The sender connection is auto generated from the cluster receiver information. So you need to make sure that your cluster receiver has the hostname of the receiver, the port of the receiver and the cluster / name list for which it is to be used.

Question 73: MSCS cluster asymmetry in specs

We're building an acceptance environment: Windows 2003, WBIMB6 and WMQ6.

MSCS Clustering: configuration manager and brokers are on same machines.
Active: passive configuration.

The hardware specifications of each machine in the proposed cluster are different. Will a cluster hold together provided the software requirements are satisfied?

A: Generally speaking, one wants a node that has failed over to run at the same capacity as it had before it failed over.

A reduction of capacity in a failed over state will presumably have measurable business impact. This business impact should presumably be large enough to justify a full capacity failover machine.

Sometimes management has to learn these things the hard way, rather than by reading a document that clearly spells it out. In other words, it is probably a false economy to purchase failover machines that are not the same capacity as the primary machines.

Technically, I would expect that MSCS would be capable of preserving a cluster across two machines that are not physically alike. Doing so would increase the risk of MSCS failing in subtle ways at inappropriate times, however.

Question 74: Clustering and saveqmgr

The file that is generated by saveqmgr has the channels as one of the last things in the file.

When a QM joins a cluster, does it publish the information for objects that were already marked in the cluster?

Example:

```
define qlocal(Q1) cluster(A)
define channel(TO.ME) chltype(CLUSRCVR)
CONNAME(somewhere) CLUSTER(A)
define channel(TO.THEM) chltype(CLUSSDR)
CONNAME(somewhere) CLUSTER(A)
```

Am I correct to assume that A is also published when the repository is informed of this QM?

A: I believe that the local information gets put first into the local cluster repository.

The information in the local repository gets then sent when you create/start the cluster sender to the cluster repository. And regardless, there's no validation on the CLUSTER or CLUSNL parameters, other than length and characters.

So even if there isn't a CLUSTER anywhere named "Wayne", I can share a queue in the "Wayne" cluster.

Question 75: Untrusted cluster members

My department operates QMGR1 on BOX1 and QMGR2 on BOX2 and another department operates QMGR3 on BOX3. All boxes run W2K and are on the same domain and all are using v6 of the MQ software. Our queue managers are administered by a local user mqadminA and their queue manager is administered by a domain user mqadminB. All three queue managers are in a cluster CLSTR1. For legal reasons, we have to keep our departments as separate as possible and for political reasons we have to use a cluster setup.

The problem is that if you have the authority to administer one queue manager in the cluster, you apparently have the authority to administer all of them. I want to be able to prevent the other department from being able to administer the queue managers that we're responsible for. Our queue managers are administered by a local user on each box and their queue managers are administered by a single domain user.

I can use MQ Explorer to remotely connect to their queue managers and make changes even though I am not in the administrators or mqm group on their boxes. And I know they can do the same to ours. How can I prevent them from making changes to our queue managers?

A: Try limiting their access to your cluster. Set a mcauser on the cluster receiver. Allow only connect display inquire and put access to that user. Here are some suggested steps to follow:

Create a separate cluster-receiver for the other department to connect to.

Set the MCAUSER on the new cluster-receiver to the domain user that they use.

Set the permissions for that user for my queue manager to +setall +connect +inq.

Set the permissions for the
SYSTEM.CLUSTER.COMMAND.QUEUE and
SYSTEM.DEAD.LETTER.QUEUE to +setall +put.

Set any queues the other department needs to put to +setall +put

Remove SYSTEM.ADMIN.SVRCONN channels from your qmgrs
and if there are any SVRCONN channels on your qmgrs add
mcauser as "nobody". Be careful and make sure that no
applications are using these svrconn channels.

Question 76: Cluster not seeing all queues

I have added a queue manager to a cluster; this qmgr is a cluster repository. The first repository seems to know about the new queue manager and sees all qclusters . I have the channel sat correct and starting, however, I still don't see all queues from the full repository qmgr I added. Also, I noticed an error in event viewer about the old repository which I deleted, somewhere it is still looking at the old repository. What step could I have missed?

A: You need to perform following tasks:

"forceremove" the old (deleted) repository from the remaining repository (not the new one).

Stop the cluster receiver mode (quiesce/force/terminate) on the new repository (other cluster members may still have the old ip/port on their cluster senders). The receiver MUST end up in stopped status.

Check that all the senders to the receiver have indeed stopped, if not, stop them manually again with mode terminate. You should refresh the cluster in the current sender qmgr.

Start the cluster receiver on the new repository.

Question 77: WMQ Client "get" from clustered queue

Qmgr-A on Machine A and Qmgr-B Machine B are in the same cluster and each Queue Manager has their own clustered local queue .

Can my WMQ Client program running on Machine C do a "get" from either of these clustered local queues? Do I have to code the logic in my WMQ Client application to connect to each of these queues?

A: "NO". An MQ app can only GET from qlocals on the qmgr it is connected to. One of the main points of MQ is that applications do not have to know where the queue they are 'putting' to is.

Most people would put QMgr A on the same machine as an instance of your client application and then use server bindings and Qmgr B on the same machine as another instance of your client application and use server bindings. Afterwhich, you can then have other applications connect to Qmgr C and PUT messages there.

You have to code the logic in your WMQ Client application. Your application has to connect to one QMgr and then is able to read from local queues. To read the same queue on another QMgr, the application has to connect to the other QMgr.

Question 78: Clustering design issue

We have two messages broker queue managers running hot/hot and a third queue manager which would run hot/cold. Veritas clustering would be used.

Is it possible to cluster the two message broker queue managers along with the third queue manager which would be clustered via Veritas? This queue manager would be shared between the hot/standby servers. Veritas tasks would be defined to stop/start MQ in the event of failover, etc.

Are there any implications with this approach?

A: You need to consider Veritas clustering completely separately from MQ clustering. They do different things, and are not affected by each other at all.

The only difference between a hot/hot and a hot/cold scenario in Veritas or other hardware clustering is that something is already running on the "cold" box in a hot/hot scenario. That is, in your case you have three hot/cold setups. It's just that the cold part of two of those setups is also the hot part of another: A->B, B->A, C->D.

Again, this doesn't affect MQ clustering at all. You can cluster A, B and C qmgrs and not even know if any of them are in a hardware cluster.

Your scenario is feasible. It's fairly common.

Be sure the machines that host the Hot/Hot setup are capable of running both sets of services at full capacity. This usually means you want them to be about two and a half times as big as they need to be for one set.

Question 79: MQ 5.3 Qmgr in an MQ 6.0 Cluster

When I try to add an MQ 5.3 Queue Manager to an MQ 6.0 Explorer in a different computer with the purpose of adding it from the Explorer to a Cluster, it says "Queue SYSTEM.MQEXPLORER.REPLY.MODEL is not defined."

How should I handle this situation?

A: Simply create the model queue like SYSTEM.MQSC.REPLY.QUEUE and you should be fine.

Question 80: Deftype

One of the PR queue managers dropped out of the cluster for no apparent reason. I opened a PMR with IBM and the response came back "you need manually-defined CLUSSDR channels between all FR's in the cluster."

From any of my FR's, I see some of the other FR queue managers with DEFTYPE(CLUSSDRA) <automatic sender definition>. If I now add manual definitions to connect these FRs, will the automatic definitions go away on their own? Do I need to stop/start channels? Or do I use REFRESH CLUSTER?

A: Defining a manual cluster sender channel (DEFTYPE=CLUSSDR), where an auto-defined cluster sender channel (DEFTYPE=CLUSSDRA) already exists, will turn the existing CLUSSDRA into a CLUSSDRB.

Manually defined cluster sender channels act as a kind of bootstrap and their definitions are overridden by cluster receiver definitions from remote partner queue managers. They should ALWAYS be directed at full repositories. Partial repositories use manual cluster senders to join a cluster and full repositories use manual cluster channels to identify other full repositories that they wish to share their repository info with. There are three types of cluster sender channel:

CLUSSDR: A cluster-sender channel from an explicit definition. No cluster receiver definition has been received from the partner queue manager.

CLUSSDRA: A cluster-sender channel by auto-definition alone. A cluster receiver definition has been received from the partner queue manager and used to create an auto-defined channel.

CLUSSDRB: A cluster-sender channel by auto-definition and an explicit definition. A cluster receiver has been received from the partner queue manager and used to override the manual definition with an auto-defined channel.

Cluster queue managers based on a local cluster receiver channel definition have a DEFTYPE of CLUSRCVR.

Here's what is going on when you create your cluster:

Define clusrcvr TO.QM0 on QM0.
   * "DIS CLUSQMGR(*) DEFTYPE" on QM0 returns
   - CLUSQMGR=QM0, DEFTYPE=CLUSRCVR
   * "DIS CLUSQMGR(*) DEFTYPE" on QM1 returns
   - none
   * "DIS CLUSQMGR(*) DEFTYPE" on QM2 returns
   - none

Define clusrcvr TO.QM1 on QM1.
   * "DIS CLUSQMGR(*) DEFTYPE" on QM0 returns
   - CLUSQMGR=QM0, DEFTYPE=CLUSRCVR
   * "DIS CLUSQMGR(*) DEFTYPE" on QM1 returns
   - CLUSQMGR=QM1, DEFTYPE=CLUSRCVR
   * "DIS CLUSQMGR(*) DEFTYPE" on QM2 returns
   - none

Define clussdr TO.QM0 on QM1.
   * "DIS CLUSQMGR(*) DEFTYPE" on QM0 returns
   - CLUSQMGR=QM0, DEFTYPE=CLUSRCVR
   * "DIS CLUSQMGR(*) DEFTYPE" on QM1 returns
   - CLUSQMGR=QM1, DEFTYPE=CLUSRCVR
   - CLUSQMGR=QM0, DEFTYPE=CLUSSDR
   * "DIS CLUSQMGR(*) DEFTYPE" on QM2 returns
   - none

The channel TO.QM0 on QM1 will be started automatically. QM1 sends its cluster receiver definition to QM0. QM0 uses that definition to auto-define a cluster sender to QM1.
   * "DIS CLUSQMGR(*) DEFTYPE" on QM0 returns
   - CLUSQMGR=QM0, DEFTYPE=CLUSRCVR
   - CLUSQMGR=QM1, DEFTYPE=CLUSSDRA
   * "DIS CLUSQMGR(*) DEFTYPE" on QM1 returns
   - CLUSQMGR=QM1, DEFTYPE=CLUSRCVR
   - CLUSQMGR=QM0, DEFTYPE=CLUSSDR
   * "DIS CLUSQMGR(*) DEFTYPE" on QM2 returns
   - none

The channel TO.QM1 on QM0 will be started automatically. QM0 sends its cluster receiver definition to QM1. QM1 uses that definition to auto-define a cluster sender to QM0. As there is already a cluster queue manager object with DEFTYPE(CLUSSDR), that one is overridden and becomes a CLUSSDRB.

```
* "DIS CLUSQMGR(*) DEFTYPE" on QM0 returns
- CLUSQMGR=QM0, DEFTYPE=CLUSRCVR
- CLUSQMGR=QM1, DEFTYPE=CLUSSDRA
* "DIS CLUSQMGR(*) DEFTYPE" on QM1 returns
- CLUSQMGR=QM1, DEFTYPE=CLUSRCVR
- CLUSQMGR=QM0, DEFTYPE=CLUSSDRB
* "DIS CLUSQMGR(*) DEFTYPE" on QM2 returns
- none
```

Define clussdr TO.QM0 on QM2.
```
* "DIS CLUSQMGR(*) DEFTYPE" on QM0 returns
- CLUSQMGR=QM0, DEFTYPE=CLUSRCVR
- CLUSQMGR=QM1, DEFTYPE=CLUSSDRA
* "DIS CLUSQMGR(*) DEFTYPE" on QM1 returns
- CLUSQMGR=QM1, DEFTYPE=CLUSRCVR
- CLUSQMGR=QM0, DEFTYPE=CLUSSDRB
* "DIS CLUSQMGR(*) DEFTYPE" on QM2 returns
- CLUSQMGR=QM0, DEFTYPE=CLUSSDR
```

Define clusrcvr TO.QM2 on QM2.
```
* "DIS CLUSQMGR(*) DEFTYPE" on QM0 returns
- CLUSQMGR=QM0, DEFTYPE=CLUSRCVR
- CLUSQMGR=QM1, DEFTYPE=CLUSSDRA
* "DIS CLUSQMGR(*) DEFTYPE" on QM1 returns
- CLUSQMGR=QM1, DEFTYPE=CLUSRCVR
- CLUSQMGR=QM0, DEFTYPE=CLUSSDRB
* "DIS CLUSQMGR(*) DEFTYPE" on QM2 returns
- CLUSQMGR=QM0, DEFTYPE=CLUSSDR
- CLUSQMGR=QM2, DEFTYPE=CLUSRCVR
```

The channel TO.QM0 on QM2 will be started automatically. QM2 sends its cluster receiver definition to QM0. QM0 uses that definition to auto-define a cluster sender to QM2.
```
* "DIS CLUSQMGR(*) DEFTYPE" on QM0 returns
- CLUSQMGR=QM0, DEFTYPE=CLUSRCVR
- CLUSQMGR=QM1, DEFTYPE=CLUSSDRA
- CLUSQMGR=QM2, DEFTYPE=CLUSSDRA
* "DIS CLUSQMGR(*) DEFTYPE" on QM1 returns
- CLUSQMGR=QM1, DEFTYPE=CLUSRCVR
- CLUSQMGR=QM0, DEFTYPE=CLUSSDRB
```

* "DIS CLUSQMGR(*) DEFTYPE" on QM2 returns
- CLUSQMGR=QM0, DEFTYPE=CLUSSDR
- CLUSQMGR=QM2, DEFTYPE=CLUSRCVR

The channel TO.QM2 on QM0 will be started automatically.
QM0 sends its cluster receiver definition to QM2. QM2 uses
that definition to auto-define a cluster sender to QM0. As
there is already a cluster queue manager object with
DEFTYPE(CLUSSDR), that one is overridden and becomes a
CLUSSDRB.
* "DIS CLUSQMGR(*) DEFTYPE" on QM0 returns
- CLUSQMGR=QM0, DEFTYPE=CLUSRCVR
- CLUSQMGR=QM1, DEFTYPE=CLUSSDRA
- CLUSQMGR=QM2, DEFTYPE=CLUSSDRA
* "DIS CLUSQMGR(*) DEFTYPE" on QM1 returns
- CLUSQMGR=QM1, DEFTYPE=CLUSRCVR
- CLUSQMGR=QM0, DEFTYPE=CLUSSDRB
* "DIS CLUSQMGR(*) DEFTYPE" on QM2 returns
- CLUSQMGR=QM0, DEFTYPE=CLUSSDRB
- CLUSQMGR=QM2, DEFTYPE=CLUSRCVR

Question 81: Cluster repository

We run the MQ cluster for several of our apps that share queue functionality. We are planning cut-over strategy to our new hardware when a question came up about repository constraints. In a single cluster we need at least 2 repositories, but could have more or in a single cluster there can only exist 2 repositories, never more then two. Which is better?

A: In a single cluster you need at least one full repository. You can have as many full repositories as you like. Rarely can you get any benefit from having more than two full repositories.

Full repository queue managers should be highly available and highly reachable from all queue managers in the cluster. In some network configurations, those two reasons may provide some benefit from having more than two full repositories in a single cluster. Not much else will.

And if you do have more than 2 repository managers, then each repository manager must have a manually defined CLUSSDR to every other repository.

From the Clustering Manual

Quote:

The full repositories republish the publications they receive through the manually-defined CLUSSDR channels, which must point to other full repositories in the cluster. You must make sure that a publication received by any full repository ultimately reaches all the other full repositories. You do this by manually defining CLUSSDR channels between the full repositories. The more interconnection of full repositories you have, the more robust the cluster is.

Question 82: Clustering vs Remote Q definition

If we can cluster different Q Managers residing geographically in different boxes, then why do we use Remote Queue Definition? We can cluster the Queue Manager and treat the Queue as a local Queue!

A: The point of MQ is to connect queue managers residing geographically in different boxes. It's marketed as a better way to communicate between geographically separate boxes than native TCP/IP.

You can never treat a QCLUSTER or QREMOTE as a QLOCAL.

From an application point of view, there is no difference between a QCLUSTER and a QREMOTE. But there is a single, HUGE, difference between both of those and a QLOCAL. You can only GET from QLOCALs.

Whether or not to Cluster queue managers or connect them using standard channels is an infrastructure decision and not a developer decision.

Clustering is not well suited for a lot of infrastructure layouts or network topologies. Conversely, it is well suited for other infrastructure layouts and network topologies.

The basic principle of using CLUSTER is to achieve load balancing among many queue managers. It is usually better to use standard channel connections unless there are specific reasons to use Clustering.

Question 83: Cluster problem

I have created a cluster of 3 queue managers (QM1, QM2, QM3) and all the queue managers are on the local Windows machine.

QM1 and QM2 hold the repository. I connected QM3 to the QM1 repository queue manager. When I created a local queue in QM3, it was visible to QM1 and QM2 and when I created a local queue in QM1, it was visible to QM2 and QM3 . The problem now is when I created a local queue in QM2, it was visible to QM1 but not to QM3. Later when I changed QM3 to repository queue manager, the queue was visible. Why is this so?

A: Queue managers that are not full repositories (FR) only contain details of queues that they think they need. Rules for partial repository (PR) updating & clean up are in the manual. Hence if you add a queue to a PR both of the FR get details because they hold everything. You add a queue to a FR, the PR will only take the details on first use assuming throughout the queues are shared in the cluster.

If you repeat the sequence, leaving QM3 as a PR, connect to it & open the clustered queue, you'll then see the details on QM3 because it's been used & QM3 will have obtained the details it need to use it.

Functioning as designed!

Question 84: Workload balancing MRU channel

I'm reading some of the new V6 Workload stuff.

The manual says:

"This queue manager attribute specifies the maximum number of outbound cluster channels. The value must be in the range 1 through 999 999 999. The initial default value is 999 999 999."

What is this all about and how does this work?

A: Consider a situation where you have a small "client/branch" machine that's sending messages to a datacenter which has 100 servers, any of which might do the work.

[All 101 qmgrs in the same cluster]

You do not want your low-powered box running 100 channels/100 sockets as it sends the work into the datacenter.

So setting the MRUC to 10 will mean that it will only start 10 channels, it doesn't matter which of the 100 machines it goes to but it will only ever cycle the messages round 10 of them.

The default of 999999999 means that all of the back ends will be used which is equivalent to the V5.3 behavior.

Check "Task 15" in Advanced Workload Balancing Tasks in the clusters book.

Question 85: Differentiating clusters

What is the difference between a queue that is in the cluster and queue that is not in the cluster?

A: The only difference between a queue that is in the cluster and queue that is not in the cluster is the "cluster" attribute of the queue.

So use mqsc on each queue manager in the cluster as such:

```
Code:
def qlocal(MY.QUEUE.NAME) cluster(MY.CLUSTER.NAME)
```

Then you will see in MQ Explorer that there are 3 queues with the name "MY.QUEUE.NAME" on each queue manager - one QLOCAL and two QCLUSTERS (one for each, including the qlocal).

When doing the MQOPEN, just issue the MQOPEN using the name "MY.QUEUE.NAME"

If you want to be sure that all the messages you send go to ONE queue in the cluster, then use the MQOO_BIND_ON_OPEN.

If you want to be sure that all the messages you send go to SEVERAL queues in the cluster, then use the MQOO_BIND_NOT_FIXED.

Question 86: Removing qmgr from cluster

We are using WMQ 6.0.1 on an XP platform. I am removing a partial repository queue manager from a cluster as follows:

```
Suspend the qmgr from the cluster
Remove CLUSRCVR from cluster
Stop CLUSRCVR channel
Stop CLUSSDR channel
Delete both CLUSRCVR & CLUSSDR
```

When I go back to my remaining full repository qmgrs, I still see the removed qmgrs cluster queues listed (i.e. when I dis qc(*)).

To resolve this, I plan to force remove the old cluster member with queues set to yes. Will I have an issue here?

A: I would remove the objects (Queues) before any Channels. This way, the information is sent out to the full repositories, to "clean up".

Question 87: Cluster sender to a full repository qmgr

I heard a different scenario of the cluster at my friend's client's place.

Generally, we use one cluster sender pointing to any one of the full repository within the cluster and one cluster serving as receiver channel.

I have seen a different scenario when two cluster senders pointing to full repos1 and full repos2 are used. For example, QM1 and QM2 are the full repository queue managers and QM3 is a partial and want to join in the cluster. QM3 has a cluster receiver (TO.QM3), cluster sender1 (TO.QM1) and cluster sender2 (TO.QM2).

Why do we need two senders which are in the same cluster?

A: This is straight from the Clustering Manual:

"Using REFRESH CLUSTER(cluster name) REPOS(YES) specifies that in addition to the default behavior, objects representing full repository cluster queue managers are also refreshed. This option may not be used if the queue manager is itself a full repository. If it is a full repository, you must first alter it so that it is not a full repository for the cluster in question. The full repository location will be recovered from the manually defined CLUSSDR definitions. After the refresh with REPOS(YES) has been issued the queue manager can be altered so that it is once again a full repository, if required."

See how they said "The full repository location will be recovered from the manually defined CLUSSDR definitions." If you have more than 1 cluster sender channel defined from the partial to the full, and you issue REFRSH CLUSTER REPOS (YES), the partial will try and reintroduce itself to the cluster via both FRs. This might be a benefit if FR1 is temporarily down when you issue the REFRESH with the REPOS(YES), or when you introduce the partial for the very first time.

The manually defined cluster sender channel is only ever used the very first time a partial joins a cluster or when REPOS(YES) is used, never otherwise. So if you see these two scenarios happening while FR1 is N/A, then maybe, maybe (since its not clearly documented), having a manually defined CLUSSNDR to FR2 as well would help. At no other time are the manually defined CLUSSNDR channels used.

I would just have the one manual CLUSSNDR channel as the manual says. Aim it at the FR that is available. If FR1 is N/A and you have to add a QM to the cluster or REFRESH CLUSTER REPOS(YES) at that exact moment, just make sure you have a single CLUSSNDR aimed at FR2.

Having two (2) manually defined CLUSSNDRs is not needed in my opinion. Remember, as soon as a partial successfully joins the cluster, it will create Automatic Cluster Senders to *both* FRs, even though you only have one (1) manually defined one.

Question 88: QM as member of two clusters

How can I make a queue manager a member of two clusters? How can I communicate between the two clusters with the help of the common queue manager?

A: Look into the CLUSNL attribute of the queue manager. A queue manager can also be a member of more than one cluster without using CLUSNL by using separate channels for each cluster. If the CLUSNL attribute is used, you need it to set up for the channel - not for the QMgr (QMgrs only have a REPOSNL attribute, if they are repositories for more than one cluster).

To intercommunicate between two clusters (let's say CL1 and CL2) you need the following:

A q definition (e. g. alias q) which is a member of CL1 and points to a target queue in CL2

Another q definition (e. g. alias q) which is a member of CL2 and points to a target queue in CL1

Sample:
```
qmgr QM1 (member of CL1)
qmgr QM2 (member of CL2)
gateway qmgr QMGW (member of CL1 and CL2)

local q Q1 on QM1 (member of CL1)
local q Q2 on QM2 (member of CL2)

alias q Q12 on QMGW (member of CL1) with base q Q2
alias q Q21 on QMGW (member of CL2) with base q Q1
```

Remember, the queues Q12 and Q21 must be defined with DEFBIND(NOTFIXED) (otherwise the target will be only resolved to qs local to qmgr QMGW).

In the scenario described above, it must be defined with DEFBIND(NOTFIXED)! Otherwise the alias queues Q12 and Q21 would not resolve to the queues Q1 and Q2!

This is because the queues are not local to the QMgr QMGW (where the queues Q12 and Q21 reside).

You'll find the description in the manual "Queue Manager Clusters", chapter 4 "How does queue manager clusters work" and it does not depend on the application's architecture: "When you open a queue you need to set DEFBIND to either (NOTFIXED) or (QDEF) because if it is left as the default (OPEN) the queue manager will resolve the alias definition to the bridge queue manager that hosts it, and the bridge will not forward the message on"

Question 89: Message destination algorithm

According to WebSphere MQ Queue Managers Clusters manual that states:

"Suitability is based on the state of the channel including any priority you might have assigned to the channel, and also the availability of the queue manager and queue. The algorithm uses a round-robin approach to finalize its choice between the suitable queue managers."

What are these steps in choosing a destination for the message by default?

A: Below is the round robin algorithm which WebSphere MQ uses by default.

Algorithm: The steps in choosing a destination for a message:

If a queue name is specified, eliminate queues that are not PUT enabled. Eliminate remote instances of queues that do not share a cluster with the local queue manager. Eliminate remote CLUSRCVR channels that are not in the same cluster as the queue.

If a queue manager name is specified, eliminate queue manager alias' that are not PUT enabled. Eliminate remote CLUSRCVR channels that are not in the same cluster as the local queue manager.

If the result above contains the local instance of the queue, choose it.

If the message is a cluster PCF message, eliminate any queue manager you have already sent a publication or subscription to.

If only remote instances of a queue remains, choose Resumed queue managers over Suspended ones.

If more than one remote instance of a queue remains, include all MQCHS_INACTIVE and MQCHS_RUNNING channels.

If less than one remote instance of a queue remains, include all MQCHS_BINDING, MQCHS_INITIALIZING, MQCHS_STARTING, and MQCHS_STOPPING channels.

If less than one remote instance of a queue remains, include all MQCHS_RETRYING channels.

If less than one remote instance of a queue remains, include all MQCHS_REQUESTING, MQCHS_PAUSED and MQCHS_STOPPED channels.

If more than one remote instance of a queue remains and the message is a cluster PCF message, choose locally defined CLUSSDR channels.

If more than one remote instance of a queue remains to any queue manager, choose channels with the highest NETPRTY to each queue manager.

If more than one remote instance of a queue remains, choose the least recently used channel.

Note that if you have a cluster where all the channels are INACTIVE, and you put 1000 messages into the cluster and there are 2 queues for it, odds are you will not get a 500/500 split. One of the channels will start first, and until the second channel starts (don't worry it will), the algorithm will put all the messages to the first channel. As soon as the second channel is up, from that point forward, the algorithm will round robin the remainder of the 1000 messages.

If you put another 1000 message batch, and the channels are still running, then you will see exactly 500 go to 1 and 500 go to the other.

Question 90: ReplyToQueueManager

We have a cluster of Queue Managers A and B and another cluster of Queue Managers B and C. B participates in both clusters.

The client application connects A and sends messages to C via B. There is a local queue in C that is cluster shared in B and C and there is an alias of this queue in B that is clustered shared in A and B.

The server application connects C, processes the message and sends the reply.

Ideally, we want the client application to submit blank as ReplyToQueueManager and then MQ to set ReplyToQueueManager=B, not A as we have a communication between C and B, not between C and A.

Is it possible and how should we configure the reply queue and/or theirs alias/remote definitions so that the server application to use ReplyToQueueManager field from the header?

Are there any Put Message Options or Open Queue Options that will force MQ to set as ReplyToQueueManager the name of the gate queue manager (B), not the queue manager that owns the reply queue (A)?

A: No, there are no such options on the put. Just make a qmgr alias in the BC cluster for qmgr A as qmgr B.

Question 91: Creating the default Cluster Sender Channel

I have two Queue Managers, one running on Windows and one on UNIX. While trying to create a cluster between these two queue managers the cluster creation fails. On examining the problem, I see that the Queue Manager on the UNIX system has the default Cluster Sender channel "SYSTEM.DEF.CLUSSDR" missing. When I try to create a Cluster Sender channel it asks me to give the default attribute and since the default cluster channel missing, I cannot manually create a cluster sender channel.

Is there a way I can create this default Cluster Sender Channel?

A: The strmqm -c creates the default objects.

Question 92: A doubt about cluster command queue

The manual describes the use of
SYSTEM.CLUSTER.COMMAND.QUEUE as:

Quote:

Each queue manager in a cluster has a local queue called
SYSTEM.CLUSTER.COMMAND.QUEUE. This queue is used to
carry messages to the full repository. The queue manager uses
this queue to send any new or changed information about itself
to the full repository queue manager and to send any requests for
information about other queue managers. This queue is normally
empty.

As far as I know, messages meant for full repository queue may
have a certain format that needs to be generated by the
command server manning the command queue. So, command
queue may act as an intermediary between the Command Server
and the transmit queue.

Now, how can this queue be use to "send" any message when it is
a local queue? The messages are actually sent by the
SYSTEM.CLUSTER.TRANSMIT.QUEUE.

A: The document isn't exactly clear on this. As an example:

If you have two qmgrs, say QMP and QMF, and QMP is a partial
repository and QMF is a full repository, then when you issue a
command to QMP to define a queue which is in the cluster, what
QMP does is send a "define" command to the command queue
SYSTEM.CLUSTER.COMMAND.QUEUE at QMF via the
SYSTEM.CLUSTER.TRANSMIT.QUEUE on QMP.

QMP "knows" to send the message to QMF because you defined a
channel with the same cluster name, of type CLUSSDR which
"points" to QMF.

I hope that makes sense.

Question 93: Suspend cluster membership

We're looking for a more intelligent method of upgrading, including saving the file system this time, but we are unsure about the cluster.

Our normal course of action for previous upgrades is to:

Run saveqmgr to backup object definitions.
Leave the cluster (if the qmgr is full repos - we nominate another qmgr in the cluster to temporarily assume full repos duties).
Uninstall MQ completely - including deletion of the file system folders-install MQ.
Rebuild QMgr and objects from the define statements.
Rejoin the cluster

When planning to migrate from V5.3 to V6, should I plan on suspending the membership of a QMgr on this Windows installation? Does it matter that the QMgr is a full or partial repository in the cluster?

A: Suspending a QMgr during upgrade does not hurt but you don't have to rebuild the QMgr. Just do the following:

Suspend your QMgr (if you want).
End the QMgr.
Store the data path with tar or what you like.
Uninstall MQ version 5.3 (if you like, it is mostly not necessary).
Install MQ version 6..
Start the QMgr.

But do not:

Delete the file system folders.
Rebuild QMgr and objects.

MQ preserves the configuration, permissions and data when you remove the installation. After reinstallation of MQ same or higher version the configuration, permissions and data will be available again. If you have trouble, stop the QMgr, reinstall the old MQ version, restore the data paths from the backup, and start the QMgr.

But when you delete the file system folders (/var/mqm) and recreate the QMgr, you will get another QMgr. Although the name and configuration of the QMgr will be the same, on the cluster repository you will see two QMgrs with the same name - but a different QMgr ID!

A suspended queue manager may still receive work from the cluster. You are better off completely removing it from the cluster rather than suspending, particularly if you are going to delete the qmgr.

Lastly, you absolutely should upgrade your FRs first to ensure that you do not corrupt your v5 cluster repository with v6 objects.

Question 94: MQ fail over testing

I am working with MQ cluster with 2 nodes:
QM1 is on node1.
QM2 is on node2; both are cluster with CLUST1.

QM3 is on another node without cluster.

If I send some 5 messages to one of the queue in the cluster from the QM3, does it share those messages to between the 2 queue managers or it will go only one QM?

Do I need to configure for load share in between the 2 QM's on the cluster?

A: Though QM3 is not member of a MQ cluster, you have to define non-cluster channels between QM3 and/or QM1 and QM2. You also need remote queues, to define a way to a queue on QM1 or QM2. These remote queues are fix definitions.

To share the load, you have to add QM3 to the cluster CLUST1. You also need a cluster queue (instead of a remote queue) on QM1 AND QM2. These queues must have the same name and should have the same attributes (DEFBIND etc.). Then MQ will share the load between QM1 and QM2 (for messages, which come from QM3).

Question 95: Message retrieve in a MQ cluster

I have MQ CLuster setup in a round robin fashion. I have Cluster queue with same name created on two servers so messages go to one of the two MQ Servers and are processed from there.

Are these messages stored in the repository or individually on each of the machines? What if one server goes down for some reason, can the messages which were in that machine before it went down be retrieved from other machine in Cluster with full repository ?

A: The cluster repository only holds cluster information about cluster queue managers and cluster queues; it does not store application messages.

Messages are stored in the local queues you defined in every queue manager. If one of them is down, you can not access the messages.

The only setup where this is possible is shared queues on z/OS environment and WAS 6.0 internal JMS provider with DB persistency store.

Question 96: Remote queue pointing to a cluster queue

I have a gateway Qmgr not part of the cluster. It has a remote queue definition to a qmgr(QM1) inside the cluster, with the RName pointing to a cluster queue not hosted by QM1.

When I send data to the remote queue on the Gateway, the messages ends up in the DLQ of QM1 with a 2085 RC.

I can do a dis qcluster(*) on QM1 and see the clustered queues. I can log on to the QM1 server and perform an amqsput to the cluster queue with no problem.

Can you remote queue a message to a clustered queue not owned by the receiving Qmgr?

A: You need to set your cluster queue in such a way that it is addressable on the gateway. What you experience is working as designed.

Here is a suggestion: Set up a qmgr alias with values like:

```
Code:
def qr(clustername) rqmname(' ')
```

Now set up a remote queue that sends the message to queue(X) on qmgr(clustername) on the gateway. The name resolution will be no qmgr name on the gateway and that would translate to the clustered queue(X) in round robin where they are hosted.

Question 97: Load balancing

Is there a way in MQ queue manager were I can automatically start posting messages to Q-2 if Q-1 is overloaded or the destination of Q1 is slow in reading the messages?

A: The way to go about it is improve performance or run another instance of the receiving application. Calculate/Estimate your maximum throughput, double it to make sure, and design your application logic and WMQ environment to fit the requirements. No need for another queue, WMQ can take the heat, it's usually the application or some tunable parm that's at fault; you can dynamically raise as many instances as you wish.

If Q1 and Q2 are getting equal # of messages, but one of the 2 queues is backing up, don't attack the problem by sending fewer messages there. Attack the problem by finding out why this q is being drained slower than that one.

In order to load balance you might add an event listener and set the queue instance to put disabled if the queue depth goes over x % and re-enable it if it drops under y%. In a clustered instance this would automatically redirect the messages to the other instances.

Take into consideration the following:

MQGET destructively and by order. If possible avoid getting by corrlid or msgid, if you have to, use indexing (z/OS only).

Take to heart such channel parms as BATCHSZ, BATCHINT and BATCHHB.

Avoid Java.

Avoid Clients.

Work with syncpoint and commit only, say, 10 msgs, this will increase throughput by 300% at least.

If possible use non-persistent msgs.

MQ, like any other software, has many more malfunctions and crashes when working with such high loads, this is an unavoidable but little known fact of the industry. Plan ahead to have major problems - allocate time for it, plan an active/active cluster (MSCS or such) to quickly recover.

In z/OS there are many more considerations - archiving, STGCLASSes and more. If this is relevant post so and I will try to advice.

If sending the same msg to a few locations, use distribution lists. In my experience no need to use more than one queue, it will take it. Just note its MAXDEPTH and such parms.

There are some wondrous Redbooks and support pacs with performance tests and tuning advice, you should definitely take a good look at them.

Question 98: AMQ4043 - adding remote queue to a cluster

I am trying to add a remote queue to a cluster on the same network but different machines. When connecting to the repository, I get an AMQ4043 error code. I am entering the repository in the queue manager name, and the Ip address plus port number for the connection name - x.x.x.x(pt#). My error log shows the following:

AMQ9520: Channel not defined remotely.

EXPLANATION: There is no definition of channel 'SYSTEM.ADMIN.SVRCONN' at the remote location.

ACTION: Add an appropriate definition to the remote hosts list of defined channels and
retry the operation.

Am I missing something related to this SVRCONN channel? Anything else I should look at?

A: AMQ4043 means "The Queue Manager is not available for connection."

Corrective action: Confirm the MQManager is running. If the MQManager is running on a remote computer ensure that it is configured to accept remote connections.

So make sure the runmqlsr is running and listening to the port you are attempting to connect to.

The default channel that GUI's of this nature use to connect to an MQManager is the SYSTEM.ADMIN.SVRCONN Channel and apparently, this channel is not defined on the MQManager you are trying to connect to.

If you have local access and authority to this MQManager log on and define the channel with the "define chl(SYSTEM.ADMIN.SVRCONN) chltype(SVRCONN)" command. If not contact someone who does have local access and authority to do so.

Alternatively, it will be easier if you used "runmqsc" to share the queues in the cluster instead of the GUI. I assume the hosting queue manager has been added successfully to the cluster by you and you have access privileges on the host do run "runmqsc".

Question 99: Gateway cluster

I plan to use a pair of QMs as a gateway in to a central cluster for both downstream clustered and downstream non-clustered QMs.

In the central cluster is a pair of broker machines each with a queue exposed in the cluster for load balancing purposes.

These gateway machines will use linear logging and I will do a daily backup after bringing down the queue manager.

As part of the backup, I will do a SUSPEND on the gateway QM which will load balance all downstream clustered traffic to the other gateway.

The non-clustered downstream QM can handle the outage while the backup occurs. My question relates to traffic from these non-clustered QMs destined for the broker cluster queues via the gateway.

If I do a SUSPEND before I stop the channels, will I get a cluster resolution error for incoming traffic for the broker or will they still get written to the cluster transmit queue?

Do I need to stop the channels first?

A: I would suspend first. This should redirect all cluster traffic to the other broker. Then stop all channels run rcdmqimg and finally shut down the qmgr:

- Suspend
- Stop channels
- rcdmqimg
- endmqm -i qmgr
- Do the off line backup
- Restart the qmgr
- Archive the linear logs
- Restart the channels
- Resume the qmgr in the cluster

Question 100: Failovering and load balancing at the same time

Is this possible to get a complete solution of failovering and load balancing at the same time within a MQ 5.3 2-units cluster environment? Is there a way to setup a MQ workload management algorithm to perform that type of solution?

A: You cannot construct the complete scheme without some kind of hardware-failover solution; if you use MQ Clusters only, when one of them drops the other will indeed take over all traffic, but all messages that were retained in the QM that's down, will wait in queues and not be serviced.

To implement a full scale failover+workload solution do the following:

Create two QMs on two shared drives called QM1 & QM2, so that your setup will look like this:

Machine A: QM1 up, QM2 down
Machine B: QM1 down, QM2 Up

Both QMs should be members of the same MQ cluster with two instances of the same cluster queue.

In case machine A crashes (or shutdown for maintenance), you failover QM1 to machine B, and vice versa; the MQ cluster will keep everything flowing automatically to the available QMs so that the failover will have little effect on your business processes.

Note that if either QM crashes, while it's down you still can't get the retained messages in it's queues, but the idea is that it is fairly easy to failover it to the other machine; if the QM itself is botched, then traffic flows on, but you'll have to fix the qm to get to these messages.

Websphere MQ Java/JMS: Issues relating to Websphere MQ Java API or JMS

Question 101: Configuring MQSeries to send messages to a JMS Queue

I have an MQSeries Server and a SAP Server which has a JMS service running. I need to send message from the MQSeries to the JMS Queue. In JMS queue, there is no Queue Manager and hence I cannot send the message.

What do I need in order to set up MQSeries to send messages to the JMS Queue?

A: Install the MQSeries Client on the SAP server. With that you will get the JMS for MQSeries. Configure the JNDI appropriately and reference the mq jms jar file in your code.

You need as well to program a JMS bridge between your 2 JMS providers:

- IBM Websphere MQ
- SAP

That is assuming SAP is acting as a JMS Provider and not just as a JMS client.

Question 102: QMgr has connection pool

Does QManager have a connection pool like JDBC? I have a multi-thread environment and each thread will connect and close the Qmanager. Do I need to close QManager each time? Do I need a QManager connection pool?

A: The QM can have 'n' connection handles. The number is decided when you create the QM and its default 256.

You can close the QM when done, a close would not stop the QM, it would simply free the handle that you are using.

Question 103: Start JMS using VisualAge

I use a 2000 server and I want to configure VisualAge to run jms with mqseries.

I modified JMSAdmin and configured file:

```
INITIAL_CONTEXT_FACTORY=com.ibm.ejs.ns.jndi.CNInitial
ContextFactory PROVIDER_URL=iiop://ahmed:900
```

and import all package required, edited the classpath and resources of VisualAge.

Then, I started the Persistence name server but when I try to run JMSAdmin inside VisualAge: "JNDI initialization failed, please check your JNDI settings and service"

What other steps should I have done?

A: The following steps might be useful to start JMS using VisualAge (from an IBM workshop):

Assume C:\MQSeries is your MQ Installation root path

1.   Add MQ JMS Classes:

Create a new project called MQ JMS.

Select the MQ JMS project and import the following class libraries (jar files)from the C:\MQSeries\Java\lib directory:

```
com.ibm.mq.jar
```

2.   Add MQ JMS Resources:

In addition to the MQ JMS classes, there are some additional files that are required by MQ JMS which need to be imported into VisualAge Java. The first - mqji.properties - is a properties file containing warning and error messages used by MQ JMS.

The second - JMSAdmin.config - is a configuration file used the MQ JMS Administration tool and contains the relevant settings for connecting to a namespace.

Open the MQ JMS project in a project browser. Switch to the Resource tab and add the following resources:

C:\MQSeries\Java\lib\mqji.properties
C:\MQSeries\Java\bin\JMSAdmin.config

3. Run the Installation Verification Test (IVT):

Here, we will run the Installation Verification Test (IVT) application again to verify our install. Only this time we are running it inside VisualAge Java.

Open the MQ JMS project in a project browser. Select the com.ibm.mq.jms package and then the MQJMSIVT class within that package. Right click and select Run->Check Classpath.

In the properties dialogue, click the Compute Now button to generate the classpath. The classpath should now include the following projects:

- IBM Enterprise Extension Libraries
- IBM WebSphere Test Environment

Before closing the dialogue, switch to the Program tab and add the following command line argument –no jndi so we can run it without requiring a jndi namespace to be configured.

Run the MQJMISVT.

4. Configure JMS Admin using the WebSphere Test Environment:

In the previous step we ran the IVT script in non-jndi mode. Typically, however, JMS applications will use administered objects retrieved from a namespace. The MQ JMS Administration tool - JMSAdmin - is the tool that allows us to bind JMS objects to a jndi namespace.

As was the case when configuring the JMSAdmin tool to use the WebSphere namespace, we will need to configure the JMSAdmin tool to use the WebSphere Test Environment (WTE) namespace. Again, the two key values that we need to set are the INITIAL_CONTEXT_FACTORY and the PROVIDER_URL. These properties are held in the JMSAdmin.config file which we will now modify:

a) Pen the JMSAdmin.config file using Notepad as the text editor. This file is located in the C:\IBMVJAVA\ide\project_resources\MQ JMS directory.

b) Remove the comments from the following lines: INITIAL_CONTEXT_FACTORY=com.ibm.ejs.ns.jndi.CNInitialC ontextFactory PROVIDER_URL=iiop://localhost/.

c) We need to add the relevant classes required by JMSAdmin to its classpath. In the MQ JMS project, select the JMSAdmin class within the com.ibm.mq.jms.admin package. Right click and select Run->Check Classpath. In the properties dialogue, click the Compute Now button to generate the classpath.

d) We now want to verify that the JMSAdmin tool is configured correctly. If running, stop the WebSphere adminserver. Start the WebSphere Test Environment (WTE) using: Workspace ->Tools->WebSphere Test Environment.

e)   In the WTE window, start the Persistent Name Server (PNS).

f) Once the PNS has completed startup (i.e. 'Server open for e-business' output in Console), start the JMSAdmin tool. To do this, run the JMSAdmin class located in the MQ JMS project within the com.ibm.mq.jms.admin package. You should see the prompt InitCtx> in the output area of the Console.

Note: If you receive the error message: JNDI initialization failed, check that the PNS is running and that WTE is on the JMSAdmin classpath. In addition, take a look at the JMSAdmin.config file to see that the correct properties have been set.

g) Leave the JMSAdmin application running as we will be defining some JMS Administered objects in the next step.

5.   Define the JMS Administered Objects for use by the Installation Verification Test (IVT). The IVT application

when used in jndi mode makes use of a number of administered JMS objects - a QueueConnectionFactory and a Queue, which we will need to define here.

a) Firstly we will add a JMS QueueConnectionFactory object. As shown below, in the Standard In area of the Console enter: DEFINE QCF(ivtQCF).

b) Now we need to add a JMS Queue object to the namespace. As shown below, in the Standard In areas of the Console enter: DEFINE Q(ivtQ) QUEUE(SYSTEM.DEFAULT.LOCAL.QUEUE).

c) Lets browse the context to see our newly created JMS objects. In the Standard In areas of the Console enter: DISPLAY CTX. You should now see the following output. Note: look for the JMS objects ivtQ and ivtQCF.

d) Now that we've created our JMS objects in the namespace we can stop the JMS Admin application. In the Standard In area of the Console enter: END.

6. Run the Installation Verification Test (IVT) with WebSphere Test Environment. Previously we ran the Installation Verification Test (IVT) application without using a jndi namespace.

We now want to run the IVT again but this time using a jndi namespace, which in VisualAge Java is the WebSphere Test Environment (WTE). This will require using the JMSAdmin tool to bind the relevant JMS objects in the WTE namespace.

a) Now run the IVT application but this time using jndi. Select the MQ JMS project and navigate to the MQJMSIVT class in the com.ibm.mq.jms package. Right click and select Run->Run Main with the following command line arguments:
-url iiop://localhost:900 -icf
com.ibm.ejs.ns.jndi.CNInitialContextFactory.

Question 104: JNDI initialization failed

I'm a beginner to JMS and MQ. I just installed WebSphereMQ5.3.0.2 on a Windows XP machine. While installing MQ, I installed JMS messaging service option and want to create topics and stuff using JMS.

I found out that I need to use JMSADMIN tool for this but when I try to run that tool, I got this message: "JNDI initialization failed, please check your JNDI settings and service"

The INITIAL_CONTEXT and PROVIDER_URL in the JMSADMIN.config file have the following values:

```
#INITIAL_CONTEXT_FACTORY=com.sun.jndi.ldap.LdapCtxFac
tory
#INITIAL_CONTEXT_FACTORY=com.sun.jndi.fscontext.RefFS
ContextFactory
#INITIAL_CONTEXT_FACTORY=com.ibm.ejs.ns.jndi.CNInitia
lContextFactory
#INITIAL_CONTEXT_FACTORY=com.ibm.websphere.naming.Wsn
InitialContextFactory
```

and

```
#PROVIDER_URL=ldap://polaris/o=ibm,c=us
#PROVIDER_URL=file:/C:/JNDI-Directory
#PROVIDER_URL=iiop://localhost/
```

Now, which one of them should I enable to get the JMSADMIN tool working?

A: You need to uncomment the initial Context factory you are using and its proper provider url.

As a beginner, its better to use the sun file based JNDI as it is the easiest to use in stand alone. Once you understand how it works, you'll be ready to move on to a more complex JNDI environment.

Question 105: Multiple Connects

I need to run a process to continuously poll a queue for messages. This process is triggered once in a day. My options are:

I open a queue and perform get operations on them every minute the time-check required when the process is triggered.

I should connect-get-disconnect every minute.

What is the better alternative?

A: There's nothing wrong with writing an MQ program that will run all day, every day, and keep the MQ connection open all day every day. You should program in a number of options to ensure that the MQ administrator can do what needs to be done.

It's a bad idea to write a program that will open up a connection once a minute and then close it again.

Depending on how often messages will show up in the queue, you can use a purely triggered program which will get started when a message appears on the queue and end when the queue is empty. You may also opt to use a listener-style program which will get started once and use a "wait" timeout to get messages when there are messages. Also, you can use a mixed program that will get triggered but hang around listening to the queue for a while after the queue is empty.

Question 106: MQ triggering and message listener

When should I use MQ triggering and when to use Message listener?

A: You should use triggering when you want your application triggered by an incoming message, and a listener when your application to listen for an incoming message.

Triggering suits intermittent applications, where you don't want the application to be running all the time.

Listening suits more intensive and continuous applications where you don't want the overhead of triggering and of loading the application for each message.

Listening can load-balance by simply running more threads which each listen on the same queue, this gives greater availability.

Always use MQGET with MQGMO_WAIT (and CONVERT, FIQ) in listener code. Do not repeatedly issue MQGET without a wait option or wait in your own code as this will make the design either less responsive or inefficient.

Question 107: Pcf need not login id and password

The MSOB example uses host, port and channel name to connect to MQ. Why does it not need login ID and Password?

A: MQ does not authenticate connections by asking for a username and password, ever, in any environment.

It authorizes connections based on the runtime context of the connection originator your program.

In the case of Java programs, with client connections, the runtime context is only what is available to a standard JVM with standard Java calls. This means there is no access to OS level user stores.

Question 108: MQ API vs. JMS API

I was just thinking about the pros and cons of MQ API vs. JMS API. Why should I consider one over the other?

A: Comparing performance of the Sun JMS Provider with the WebSphere MQ JMS Provider is comparing bananas to apples. It's entirely likely that the Sun JMS Provider may run faster than WebSphere MQ when Sun is doing unreliable messaging and MQ is doing persistent messaging. But unless you really understand the testing that was done, and the conditions that are being compared, you should take any such statements as pure marketing. Your own experience will be completely different.

Use JMS when you're running code in a J2EE container.

Use WMQ Java API when you're writing things that need fine grained control of WMQ.

Use your own best judgment when deciding for things that are somewhere in between.

Do not make any decisions based on performance without clear performance requirements, test plans, monitoring and analysis, and target metrics.

Question 109: Set MQPMO and MQGMO options

My old code sets the MQPMO options using Java for MQ:

```
pmo.options = MQC.MQPMO_FAIL_IF_QUIESCING |
MQC.MQPMO_SET_IDENTITY_CONTEXT | MQC.MQPMO_SYNCPOINT;
```

I am now switching the code to use JMS using Spring. In JMS, I do not see anyway to set these specific IBM MQ options. Is there a work around to set these while using JMS?

A: Here are the MQ natives to JMS mappings:

```
MQPMO_FAIL_IF_QUIESCING: see
MQConnectionFactory.setFailIfQuiesce(int) with
JMSC.MQJMS_FIQ_YES (default) and JMSC.MQJMS_FIQ_NO

MQPMO_SYNCPOINT: see connection.createSession(boolean
transacted,int
acknowledgeMode) , session.commit(),
session.rollback()

MQC.MQPMO_SET_IDENTITY_CONTEXT: JMS implementation
set
UserIdentifier(JMSXUserID) and PutApplName
(JMSXAppID) fields at send time.
```

Typically the identity cannot be set. However, check client connection using qcf.createConnection(username, passwd)

Now, the PutApplName will always be the same. It is fixed for a JMSApp. If you need something different and the target is a JMSApp, I suggest you look at the JMS header (RFH header).

Last but not least, if the source/target is not a JMS app with MQV6.0, you have qcf.setClientMatching and of course you can always use either JNDI or the URL format: "queue://QMGR/QNAME?targetClient=1" to suppress the JMS header on the send.

Question 110: Received message character set

Below is an example to send and receive message from Queue. Now, if I use Chinese symbols in message (for example: Send Chinese symbols and set 950 for CCSID) receiver must know what character encoding is used to get bytes for example to write to file.

Is there a way for the receiver to know CCSID of message?

To send:

Code:

```
    MQQueueConnectionFactory connectionFactory =
null;
    QueueConnection connection = null;
    QueueSession session = null;
    QueueSender sender = null;
    QueueReceiver receiver = null;
    Queue myQueue = null;

    try {

    connectionFactory = new
MQQueueConnectionFactory();
    connectionFactory.setHostName(hostName);
    connectionFactory.setQueueManager("QM_manager")
;
    //connectionFactory.setChannel(channelName);
//?????????
    connectionFactory.setPort(port);
    connectionFactory.setTransportType(JMSC.MQJMS_T
P_BINDINGS_MQ);
    connectionFactory.setCCSID(ccsid);
    connection =
connectionFactory.createQueueConnection();
    session = connection.createQueueSession(false,
Session.AUTO_ACKNOWLEDGE);
    myQueue = session.createQueue(queueName);
      ((MQQueue) myQueue).setTargetClient(1);
     sender = session.createSender(myQueue);
    TextMessage message =
session.createTextMessage();
```

```
          //System.out.println("ddd: " +
message.CHARSET_PROPERTY);
message.setStringProperty("JMS_IBM_Character_Set",Str
ing.valueOf(1200));
          String text = "Some text";
          message.setText(text);
          sender.send(message);
     }
     catch (Exception ex) {
        ex.printStackTrace();
     }
     finally {
        try {
           if ( sender != null ) {
              sender.close();
           }
           if ( receiver != null ) {
              receiver.close();
           }
           if ( session != null ) {
              session.close();
}
     if ( connection != null ) {
       connection.close();
      }
     }
     catch (Exception ex) {
      }
    }
  }
..................
```

To receive:

```
Code:

     MQQueueConnectionFactory connectionFactory =
null;
     QueueConnection connection = null;
     QueueSession session = null;
     QueueSender sender = null;
     QueueReceiver receiver = null;
     Queue myQueue = null;

     try {
```

```
        connectionFactory = new
MQQueueConnectionFactory();
        connectionFactory.setHostName(hostName);
        connectionFactory.setQueueManager("QM_manager")
;
        //connectionFactory.setChannel(channelName);
//?????????
        connectionFactory.setPort(port);
        connectionFactory.setTransportType(JMSC.MQJMS_T
P_BINDINGS_MQ);
        connectionFactory.setCCSID(ccsid);
        connection =
connectionFactory.createQueueConnection();
        session = connection.createQueueSession(false,
Session.AUTO_ACKNOWLEDGE);
        myQueue = session.createQueue(queueName);
          ((MQQueue) myQueue).setTargetClient(1);
          receiver = session.createReceiver(myQueue);


        JMSTextMessage recMsg = (JMSTextMessage )
receiver.receive(1);

        String recString = recMsg.getText();

    }
    catch (Exception ex) {
      ex.printStackTrace();
    }
    finally {
      try {
        if ( sender != null ) {
          sender.close();
        }
        if ( receiver != null ) {
          receiver.close();
        }
        if ( session != null ) {
          session.close();
        }
        if ( connection != null ) {
          connection.close();
        }
      }
      catch (Exception ex) {
      }
    }
  }
}
```

A: Try to observe the following:

Set the CCSID x on the qcf object. So the qmgr will know you are sending textmessages in CCSID x which may be different from the ccsid of the qmgr.

On the receiving qmgr, do nothing. JMS TextMessage does automatically a get with Convert. If the receiving application has a different CCSID than the receiving qmgr see point 1.

Make sure there is a default translation existing between the receiving qmgr CCSID and the message CCSID.

Make sure you have the full client installed and the library/jar files being pointed at are the original ones in their respective original directory otherwise you might get a CCSID conversion not supported.

Question 111: MQ error still thrown on System.err

I'm doing basic R/W operations on a queue (in binding mode) with classic MQ and no JMS. Everything is working fine except that the exception is still thrown on System.err and is displayed on the output.

E.g. If I do a 'get' on an empty queue, I get an exception with reason Code: MQException.MQRC_NO_MSG_AVAILABLE, then I will display the message "queue is empty". The output will still include the mq exception completion and reason code like this:

Loading configuration ... done
[color=red]MQJE001: Completion Code 2, Reason 2033[/color]
queue is empty.

Is there a workaround on this problem?

A: Exceptions that are thrown while a WebSphere MQ base Java application is running are also written to the log. However, an application can call the MQException.logExclude() method to prevent exceptions associated with a specific reason code from being logged. You might want to do this in situations where you expect many exceptions associated with a specific reason code to be thrown, and you do not want the log to be filled with these exceptions.

Just include this in your init code:

```
Code:
MQException.log = null;
```

Question 112: Completion Code 2, Reason 2009

I'm using a JBoss server 3.2.8.SP1 with IBM Websphere MQ Series version 5.3. I am unable to receive messages from Queue and am getting an error of "MQJE001: Completion Code 2, Reason 2009".

My J2EE Application runs in my local machine and IBM Websphere is running in another machine.

What is the reason for code 2009?

A: The main cause for reason code 2009 for a Web application is that it is leaking connections or the max connection pool value is set way too high or there is no max connection pool value, hence it is unlimited.

The default max number of channels for a queue manager is 100. Try changing it to 200. If the Web application again gets rc=2009 then you know there is a connection pool problem.

On the server where the queue manager is running, do the following to count the number of connections:

```
Code:
netstat -an | grep 1414 |wc -l
```

Question 113: Queue Enable/Disable in Java

I want MQ commands to translate into Java.

```
RUNMQSC
ALTER QLOCAL( QueueName ) GET ( ENABLED/DISABLED )
```

What are the enabled/disabled int values? I also need the inhibit values for MQQueue.setInhibitGet(?) and MQQueue.setInhibitPut(?).

A: For the enabled/disabled int values: public void setInhibitGet(int inhibit).

The int inhibit values are:

```
MQC.MQQA_GET_INHIBITED
MQC.MQQA_GET_ALLOWED
```

Question 114: A sample RFH2 header

Can you provide a sample RFH2 header ?

A: Look in your <MQ_Install_Dir>\Tools\c\include directory and you will find cmqc.h. It has everything you need.

Code:
```
*******************************************************
/
 /*  MQRFH2 Structure -- Rules and Formatting Header
2          */
 /*****************************************************
/

  typedef  struct  tagMQRFH2  MQRFH2;
  typedef  MQRFH2  MQPOINTER  PMQRFH2;

  struct tagMQRFH2 {
    MQCHAR4    StrucId;                      /*
Structure identifier */
    MQLONG     Version;                      /*
Structure version number */
    MQLONG     StrucLength;          /* Total
length of MQRFH2 including all

NameValueLength and NameValueData fields */
    MQLONG     Encoding;                     /*
Numeric encoding of data that follows  last

NameValueData field */
    MQLONG     CodedCharSetId;       /* Character
set identifier of data that follows last

NameValueData field */
    MQCHAR8    Format;                       /*
Format name of data that follows last

NameValueData field */
    MQLONG     Flags;                        /*
Flags */
    MQLONG     NameValueCCSID;       /* Character set
identifier of

NameValueData */
  };
```

```
#define MQRFH2_DEFAULT {MQRFH_STRUC_ID_ARRAY},\
                        MQRFH_VERSION_2,\
                        MQRFH_STRUC_LENGTH_FIXED_2,\
                        MQENC_NATIVE,\
                        MQCCSI_INHERIT,\
                        {MQFMT_NONE_ARRAY},\
                        MQRFH_NONE,\
                        1208
```

The RFH2 is a fixed/variable structure, where the variable portion at the end has an XML-like structure but is not an XML document per se. Certainly you can't parse it as such because of the fixed length portion on the front which helpfully contains the length of the variable section.

Question 115: Ghost Queues - delete or not to delete

Why are Ghost Queues created? Are there any effects on the Qmgr if I remove them?

A: Users should never use OS commands to modify the queue manager file tree. It would not be safe to delete files or directories associated with ghost queues.

Ghost queues were introduced in 5.2 as part of the line item to reuse resources associated with dynamic queues. This line item resulted in very significant performance improvements to the creation of both permanent dynamic and temporary dynamic queues. In order to facilitate the reuse of the queue resources the queue file location is not based upon the queue name but is of the form "!!GHOST!id1!Counter1!id2!Counter2".

The queue manager tries to keep pools of reusable queue objects associated with the model queue from which the dynamic queues were created. The size of these pools is heuristically tuned. In emergencies the pool can be emptied by deleting and redefining the model queue.

Bottom line: Don't delete them.

Question 116: MQ cluster w/ JBoss MQ

Application uses bindings to a local queue manager; clustered queue has its localq instance on a remote queue manager. Both queue managers are members of cluster. amqsput on local JBoss system is ok but not when configured for jboss jms mq.

This was their configuration file use:

```
Code:
<attribute name="QueueManagerName"></attribute>
  <attribute
name="DestinationName">CCT.TO.WCS.MQSI.IN</attribute>
```

The error:

```
"2007-01-18 16:41:41,028 WARN
[org.jboss.system.ServiceController] Problem starting
service
com.catalystwms.wsmq.jboss:service=WSMQQueueConnectio
nFactory
javax.jms.JMSException: MQJMS1006: invalid value for
queueManager: <null>at
com.ibm.mq.jms.services.ConfigEnvironment.newExceptio
n(ConfigEnvironment.java:585) at
com.ibm.mq.jms.MQConnectionFactory.setQueueManager(MQ
ConnectionFactory.java:765)"
```

How do I put to a cluster queue using JBoss MQ (version 3) ?

A: Use a qmgr alias/cluster alias. A cluster alias is a qremote that doesn't specify a RMQNAME. You can set this as the QueueManagerName attribute value.

When messages are written to the destination, then the qremote will be used and it will overwrite the name of the qremote in the MQMD with the RMQNAME value. But that RMQNAME value is blank, so the message will be load balanced in the cluster where DestinationName is the name of the clustered local queue:

Sample code:

```
<attribute
name="QueueManagerName">BROKERQM</attribute><attribut
e
name="DestinationName">CCT.TO.WCS.MQSI.IN</attribute>
```

On JBoss server queue manager:

```
Code:
DEF QR(BROKERQM)  +
      RQMNAME(' ')       +
      XMITQ(' ')              +
      RNAME(' ')
```

Now, if you are going from a non cluster qmgr to a cluster qmgr you need to be a little bit more inventive. On the non cluster qmgr, set up a cluster alias that looks like a qmgr alias and specify the cluster name as remote qmgr and the xmitq to the cluster. On the clustered receiver (gateway), set up the cluster alias as we did above (using the cluster name as qname for the rq). The messages will then load balance in the cluster.

Remember that JBoss doesn't like having the queue manager blank in the JNDI definitions. If you specify the local queue manager in that queue manager name, then you won't use the cluster. And you can't use the name of the cluster, either. So you have to create something that has a name that you can use but ensures that the queue manager name is actually empty.

Question 117: MQINQ for Java

How can I make a Java client call MQINQ (MQSeries) to get the queue depth or maximum message length from an MVS queue?

A: Here is a sample code snippet that should work for you:

```
Code:
if (hostName != null)
        {
            MQEnvironment.hostname = hostName;
            MQEnvironment.channel  = channel;
            MQEnvironment.port     = port;
        }

        MQQueueManager qMgr = new
MQQueueManager(qMgrName);

        int openOptions = MQC.MQOO_OUTPUT         |
// for put access
                         MQC.MQOO_INQUIRE         |
// check q depth
                         MQC.MQOO_INPUT_AS_Q_DEF  |
// for get access
                         MQC.MQOO_FAIL_IF_QUIESCING
;   // break on endmqm

        MQQueue outQ = qMgr.accessQueue(qName,
                                    openOptions,
                                    null,
// default q manager
                                    null,
// no dynamic q name
                                    null);
// no alternate user id

        int curDepth = outQ.getCurrentDepth();
        System.out.println("Current depth: " +
curDepth);
```

Be sure to copy the part above that has all the open option flags and then use openOptions in the accessQueue method.

Question 118: MQJMS2013 error

We have a JMS application running under WAS and binding locally to a QM (version 6.02). The application runs under a WAS account and this is part of the mqm group. I have done a 'refresh security' but we still get the MQJMS2013 error.

I can only think that "public QueueConnection createQueueConnection(java.lang.String userName, java.lang.String password)" is being called with some bogus id as a parameter that MQ doesn't know about.

Also, a series of dspmqaut commands show WAS' to have all the required security credentials. But when I run amqoamd for the QM, it only shows mqm's credentials. Is this normal or not?

A: First of all forget all about any JMS errors. They are essentially not informative and mostly serve as a container for the provider specific error: the linked error. This one has the reason code that you need to diagnose the problem.

As for authentication through WAS, it is done in the management console. You set up the authentication in JAAS and pass it as container authentication / bean authentication.

If you are using a "bindings" connection, the only user allowed to be passed is the one running the WAS process. Any other user will give you a permission error.

If you are using a "client" connection the user must authenticate on the box the qmgr lives on and have the necessary permissions to do its job. Remember that JMS requires inq + get to be able to receive messages.

As a moderate to last resort, you can switch on security events to track down exactly what user id's failing. Remember to switch them back off when investigation is complete. This will appear on SYSTEM.ADMIN.QMGR.EVENT. You can find details in the "Monitoring MQ" manual (or online equivalent). Don't forget to switch them back off when investigation is complete.

Question 119: Gracefully stopping Java MQ app

I have a Java application running on an iSeries or AS400 that reads from a MQ queue and writes to an iSeries dataQ. How can I bring it down "gracefully" or cleanly?

A: Code it to quit when the queue is empty or code it to accept a special shutdown message.

MQ Best Practice for terminating a "Get Wait Forever":

A thread / program / whatever, puts an empty message on the queue with the MQMD's Feedback set to MQFB_QUIT.

Then in your child thread that reads the queue, put the following:

```
Code:
if (msg.feedback == MQC.MQFB_QUIT)
{
    return;
    // or throw an exception - no message or time to
quit...
}
```

Question 120: java.lang.NoClassDefFoundError: com/ibm/mq/MQException

I have written a small program in Java to connect a remote queue manager from my local system. The program is an applet program. Also, I have set the connector.jar in the CLASSPATH.

When I am running the program, it's throwing the error:

```
java.lang.NoClassDefFoundError:
com/ibm/mq/MQException
at java.lang.Class.getDeclaredConstructors0(Native
Method)
at
java.lang.Class.privateGetDeclaredConstructors(Class.
java:1747)
at java.lang.Class.getConstructor1(Class.java:2063)
at java.lang.Class.newInstance3(Class.java:331)
at java.lang.Class.newInstance(Class.java:305)
at
sun.applet.AppletPanel.createApplet(AppletPanel.java:
675)
at
sun.applet.AppletPanel.runLoader(AppletPanel.java:604
)
at sun.applet.AppletPanel.run(AppletPanel.java:333)
at java.lang.Thread.run(Thread.java:568)
```

A: For applets, the MQ jars need to be in <java install>/jre/lib/ext.

Question 121: MQException always display to stderr

I have a little MQ Message browser written with Java Base API. When I use it, I always get the "MQJE001 : Code 2, reason 2033" displayed on my stderr when I reach the end of the messages list, even if I catch the MQException.

Here's a piece of my code:

```
try {
        while (true) {
            //myMessage.clearMessage();
            MQMessage myMessage = new MQMessage();
            // Retrieving is totally independant:
clear correlation and messageID indications.
            // The access is then sequential
            myMessage.correlationId = MQC.MQCI_NONE;
            myMessage.messageId     = MQC.MQMI_NONE;
            _queue.get(myMessage, gmo);
            // Cache it.
            _messages.add(myMessage);
        }

    } catch(MQException e) {
        if (e.reasonCode ==
MQException.MQRC_NO_MSG_AVAILABLE) {
            // No more message, normal end.
        } else e.printStackTrace();
    } finally {
        closeQueue();
    }
```

How do I avoid this annoying message?

A: It's a static field from MQException class:

```
Code:
MQException.log = null
```

This prevents the exception to be duplicated to the stderr.

If you just want to remove the 2033's and not all logs, a cleaner way would be:

Code:

```
MQException.logExclude(newInteger(MQException.MQRC_NO
_MSG_AVAILABLE))
```

Question 122: Message lost on single phase transaction

We are testing the transaction scenario for client connection in single mode. In our test, we got the message in transaction mode (MQC.MQGMO_SYNCPOINT ;)

Then we remove the network code before making the commit. We got a 2009 error after that but the message seems to be removed from the queue even though I didn't do a successful commit.

Is this an expected behavior or message is supposed to be removed from the queue only if a successful commit is made?

A: You won't be able to see it if it's not committed or rolled back. You may have not done anything to explicitly commit it and haven't done anything to explicitly roll back the transaction either.

If a message has been PUT or GOT in syncpoint, but not committed, then it will be in doubt. You can tell if this is case if the QDEPTH is greater than the number of visible messages.

There is a utility to resolve transactions (e.g. amqsrsvt). Check the System Admin guide.

There is also stuff in various places about default behavior for transactions with different APIs. Sometimes an abend will force an explicit commit, and a client app disappearing counts as an abend.

Question 123: MQIVP execution error

I was using the MQ sample utility MQIVP on a Sun Solaris machine to connect to a MQ queue manager on the same machine (Binding mode). When I fire the command: java MQIVP, I get an error as below:

Error: could not find libjava.so
Error: could not find Java 2 Runtime Environment.

What is the cause of that execution error?

A: You need to set your environment variables. The first error points to LD_LIBRARY_PATH or LIBPATH depending on your flavor of UNIX.

You need to append /opt/mqm/java/lib or /usr/mqm/java/lib to it.

The second will probably tell you that you did not set env var JAVA_HOME.

Question 124: Extract JMS_IBM_PUTTIME from JMS header

I am using a JMS program. I need to get both the JMS_IBM_Puttime and JMS_IBM_Putdate.

When I ran the sample JMS program supplied by IBM which maps out the header, it shows the JMS_IBM_PutTime and JMS_IBM_PutDate in the normal yyymmdd and GMT time. Is there a method to extract that so that I don't have to do the conversion from the JMStimestamp?

A: Try this code:

```
myJMSMessage.getStringProperty ("JMS_IBM_PutTime")
```

Question 125: MQ commit

I'm reading an ISeries MQ queue from a Java program located on another ISeries box as a MQ client. It's writing to a DDM DataQ located on another ISeries box. I do my MQ commit after reading the MQ and writing to the DataQ. I presume this is ok as it is working fine.

If you are reading from multiple MQ queues and writing to multiple other MQ queues, do you need a commit for each separate write or will one suffice after the end of the logic cycle?

A: You can have multiple messages in one commit. There are things to consider like the size of the logs, the size of the messages, the max uncommitted messages and the fact that you are probably not the only user of the qmgr. Hence, there are limits and reasons. I would suggest using the commit to have restart recovery points and to have them fairly close (no more than 1000) in one go.

If the messages are large, a UOW size of 1 message may be totally justified. If performance of UOW size=1 has been proven to be a performance bottleneck, then consider increasing it. Otherwise, you should keep units of work as logically connected as possible and except in cases of grouping or message aggregation/segregation, that should be 1 message = one logical action = 1 UOW.

Every time you do a commit, a certain amount of synchronous (blocking) IO occurs that hardens the transaction to disk. The idea being that if the system fails just after the commit completes then everything is updated on disk and the system will be in the correct post-commit state.

You can do a commit after every message or after a number of messages to improve performance - this is called batching or blocking. All the messages are dequeued during a single commit which gives better performance. But, there are other concerns such as database locks (two messages try to update the same row - the first message has it locked), or timeouts where perhaps you are waiting for 10 messages before the commit, but only 9 arrive - you need to timeout and commit.

Also, you should commit MQ *after* you write to the dataqueue, if the dataqueue write fails then you can rollback the MQ message and try again later with the same MQ message. If you commit before writing to the dataqueue and the write fails, it is too late to rollback MQ and the message has been effectively lost.

Question 126: Channels remaining open on QMgr

We have a problem where channels remain open on the Queue Manager after they have been closed properly by the client.

I don't know enough about JMS to spot this one but know something isn't working up properly. We are using MQ 5.3 CSD11 and the offending code is as follows:

```
private String sendMessage(String message, String
jmsType) throws NamingException, JMSException
{
log.info("Encrypted Request: " +
removeRestrictedLoggingElements(message));
//log.info("Request: " + message);
if(message.indexOf("<name>validateAndPriceOrder") !=
-1) {
log.debug("validateAndPriceOrder message.");
validateAndPriceOrderMessage = true;
}

InitialContext ic = new InitialContext();

QueueConnectionFactory queueConnectionFactory =
  (QueueConnectionFactory)ic.lookup(ApiConstants.QUEUE
_FACTORY);
Queue queue =
(Queue)ic.lookup(ApiConstants.SEND_QUEUE);
Queue receiveQueue =
(Queue)ic.lookup(ApiConstants.RECEIVE_QUEUE);

QueueConnection connection =
queueConnectionFactory.createQueueConnection();

try
{
connection.start();
//Create a queue session
QueueSession session =
connection.createQueueSession(false,
  Session.AUTO_ACKNOWLEDGE);

try{
//Send the message
QueueSender sender = session.createSender(queue);
```

```
try
{
TextMessage textMessage =
session.createTextMessage(message);

// Default: Set the priority of message to 5
textMessage.setJMSPriority(5);
// Set the reply to queue
textMessage.setJMSReplyTo(receiveQueue);
// Set the domain to 'xml' and the type to jmsType
textMessage.setJMSType("mcd://xml//" + jmsType);
// Set a usr property
textMessage.setStringProperty("ErrorCode",
"00000000");
//Send the message
sender.send(textMessage);

//Get the message id, this is used to filter the
//subsequent read of the reply to queue
String messageId = textMessage.getJMSMessageID();

return messageId;
}finally{
sender.close();
}
}finally{
session.close();
}
}
finally
{
connection.close();
}

}
```

We are running in an Application Server. What we see is that, under load, new channels are spawned on the Queue Manager until it runs out of resource. What is wrong in my application?

A: That would be because your application is not well behaved and does not always close/release correctly the resources.

In each of your final blocks, put something like:

Code:

```
finally{
  try{
     object.close();
  }catch (JMSException jmse){
    //handle the exception
  } finally {
     object = null;
  }//end finally (internal)
}//end finally external../
```

Question 127: MQJMS1112

I want to connect to an external MQQMGR as a client through a server proxy which our network department has opened for communication outside our company. I tried using the method setProxyHostName on MQQueueConnectionFactory. (I'm using jars from MQ version 5.3 and java 1.5.)

When doing this I get the following exception:
javax.jms.IllegalStateException: MQJMS1112: JMS1.1 Invalid operations for domain specific object.

How can I achieve client communication through a proxy from a java based program without installing an own Queue Manager or installing something like "MS81: WebSphere MQ internet pass-thru"?

A: You can't establish an MQ connection through an HTTP proxy server without using MQ Internet Pass Through to tunnel the MQ traffic over HTTP.

If you tunnel the MQ traffic over HTTP, then it needs to be "un-tunneled" on the other side using MQ IPT.

The setProxyHost and setProxyPort methods only apply to creating direct connections to a Broker, not for normal connections to a queue manager.

Question 128: Error 2058

I downloaded a Java program from the IBM website called "MSender".

It is a simple bit of code that allows the user to send typed lines to a queue. I have been able to run this successfully sending to a queue defined on my local workstation but I get the error "2058 - Qmgr name error" when I try to send to a remote queue & queue manager.

I opened a dos session and updated the MQSERVER environment variable to SET MQSERVER=SVRCONCHNL/TCP/PRH345 (1414). I also double checked the names of the qmgr and queue and they're correct. Also, I wrote a Perl script that does something similar and it's working without a problem.

What does error 2058 mean?

A: A 2058 means that the QMGR name you specified is not the name of the queue manager that you connected to. You could be hitting the wrong port or the queue manager name is in the wrong case.

Question 129: Can't open cluster QALIAS MQRC 2082

Here's what we have and done:

WebSphere Application Server V.6 on Linux
WebSphere MQ Client V.6.0.1.1 on Linux

Application MQPut-> [QM2->QM1]->WAS JMS

QM1 and QM2 are qmgrs in the same Cluster CL1.
Clustered QALIAS QA1 is defined on QM1 with targetQ QL1
which is defined as a clustered QLOCAL on QM2. All Qs and
Aliases have DEFBIND (NOTFIXED) because of current problem
with DEFBIND (OPEN).

Application connects to QM2 and Puts msgs on QL1.
Connected to QM1 amqsgetc QA1 happily retrieves these
messages.

When we try to get our WAS Message Driven Bean to do the
same, i.e. get msgs from QA1 on QM1, we get MQRC 2082
UNKNOWN_ALIAS_BASE_Q.

The MDB is in a built-in WAS Container so we don't have much
control over the code that is doing the MQ requests.

JMS definition is:

```
Provider=WebSphere MQ
QCF qmgr="" host="ourhost" port="1414" Transport
Type=Client Channel=SYSTEM.DEF.SVRCONN
Queue Destination Base Queue Name="QA1" Base Qmgr=""
Target Client="MQ"
```

How come JMS MDB can't open cluster QALIAS MQRC 2082?

A: You can't get from a queue that is not a QLOCAL on the
queue manager you are connected to.

That means that if you open a QALIAS for Input, then the
QALIAS must resolve to a QLOCAL on the same qmgr.

So if you need to run an MDB against a Queue that is a qlocal on QM2, then the QCF used by the Listener Port for the MDB must point to QM2.

Question 130: putQueue.put() operation taking long time

I have a Java app that listens for messages on a queue, processes them and then sends a response. It has several threads running that poll the queue using a static class with a getMessage() method. I have recently changed this class to use MQGMO_WAIT with an interval of 5 seconds.

Since this change, when I use the classes putMessage() method, it takes a few seconds to perform putQueue.put(message). Is this expected?

Here's the code associated:

```
private static int putOpenOptions =
MQC.MQOO_FAIL_IF_QUIESCING | MQC.MQOO_OUTPUT;

/**
* Gets an mq message off the queue
* @return MQMessage - cps mq message
* @throws MQException
*/
public static MQMessage getMessage() throws
MQException {
final String METHOD_NAME ="getMessage";
//LogHelper.methodEntry(PACKAGE_NAME, CLASS_NAME,
METHOD_NAME);
MQMessage returnVal = null;
returnVal = mqGetMessage();
getQueue.get(returnVal , mqGetMessageoptions());
//LogHelper.methodExit(PACKAGE_NAME, CLASS_NAME,
METHOD_NAME);
return returnVal;
}

/**
* Sets up get message options for use on get queues
* @return
*/
private static MQGetMessageOptions
mqGetMessageoptions() {
MQGetMessageOptions getMessageOptions = new
MQGetMessageOptions();
getMessageOptions.matchOptions = MQC.MQMO_NONE;
```

```
getMessageOptions.options = MQC.MQGMO_WAIT |
MQC.MQGMO_ACCEPT_TRUNCATED_MSG |
MQC.MQGMO_FAIL_IF_QUIESCING;
getMessageOptions.waitInterval = waitInterval;
return getMessageOptions;
}

/**
 * Puts return message back on to queue
 * @param message - message to send
 * @param replyToQueueName - reply queue from request
message
 * @param replyToQmgrName - reply qgmr from request
message
 * @return
 */
public static void putMessage(MQMessage message,
String replyToQueueName, String replyToQmgrName) {
final String METHOD_NAME = "putMessage";
LogHelper.methodEntry(PACKAGE_NAME, CLASS_NAME,
METHOD_NAME);
boolean success = false;
try {
// get a handle on dynamic queue each time using
replyToQueueName and replyToQmgrName
message.seek(0);
LogHelper.debug(PACKAGE_NAME, CLASS_NAME,
METHOD_NAME, "text on put message: "
+message.readString(message.getMessageLength()));
putQueue = queueManager.accessQueue(replyToQueueName,
putOpenOptions, replyToQmgrName, null, null);
putQueue.put(message);
putQueue.close();
success = true;
putQueue = null;

} catch(MQException e) {
LogHelper.error(PACKAGE_NAME, CLASS_NAME,
METHOD_NAME, e.getMessage());
e.printStackTrace();
CPSCommunicatorHelper.sendSupportEmail(PACKAGE_NAME,
CLASS_NAME, METHOD_NAME,
CPSConstants.EMAIL_SUBJECT_ERROR,
"Exception caught: " + e.getMessage(),
CPSConstants.getEmailServer(),
CPSConstants.getEmailAlertAddress());
} catch (IOException ioe){
LogHelper.error(PACKAGE_NAME, CLASS_NAME,
METHOD_NAME, ioe.getMessage());
```

```
ioe.printStackTrace();
CPSCommunicatorHelper.sendSupportEmail(PACKAGE_NAME,
CLASS_NAME, METHOD_NAME,
CPSConstants.EMAIL_SUBJECT_ERROR,
"Exception caught: " + ioe.getMessage(),
CPSConstants.getEmailServer(),
CPSConstants.getEmailAlertAddress());
}
LogHelper.methodExit(PACKAGE_NAME, CLASS_NAME,
METHOD_NAME);
//return success;
}

/**
* Create a get message
* @return MQMessage - basic get message
*/
private static MQMessage mqGetMessage() {
MQMessage message = new MQMessage();
message.messageId = MQC.MQMI_NONE;
message.correlationId = MQC.MQCI_NONE;
return message;
}
```

Also, when not using MQGMO_WAIT the putQueue.put() action is instant.

A: Create a new QueueManager object for your Puts. You can only do one operation at a time on a qmgr connection, hence the PUT doesn't happen until the GET completes.

It's best to have one connection for each thread in a multi-threaded application. Otherwise, you are single-threading your work through the single connection.

Index